Miss Apple
Letters of a Maine
Teacher in Kentucky

Eleanor W. Cunningham

ELEANOR W. CUNNINGHAM

ISBN: 1-4033-3694-6 (e-book)
ISBN: 1-4033-3695-4 (Paperback)
ISBN: 1-4033-3696-2 (Dust Jacket)

This book is printed on acid free paper.

1stBooks – rev. 07/17/02

AFFECTIONATELY DEDICATED TO

My sisters and brother,

Alice Applebee Schmidt

Jean Leighton Testerman

and

Howard Noyes Leighton

in whom I see so much of her,

and to

Dwight Fuller

Last known surviving pupil of Ethel Valentine Applebee

PREFACE

This charming account of a young schoolteacher's experience, first in her beloved Maine and then a thousand miles and a cultural divide away from home will delight anyone who has taken such adventurous steps—or wished they had. Ethel Applebee's story was recounted eighty years later by her daughter, Eleanor Cunningham, who combined long-kept family letters with historical documentation, site visits, and her own imagination of her mother's life and thoughts.

All history is personal. While we may be a schoolteacher or immigrant or ex-slave or protest marcher or parent, we each fit into the larger scheme of history through our individual situations and the personal choices we make within the context of our own time and place. What do we leave to indicate our time on earth, our mark on society, our legacy? Perhaps photographs, recipes, holiday traditions, words of wisdom, faith or humor, children and grandchildren, a family home, a gravestone inscription, a mention in a local newspaper…

It is difficult to understand our place in history while we are in the process of living it. There is no perspective. Perhaps the best we can do is to leave hints of our lives for others to tie together and interpret, and to instill in our families the importance of preserving these pieces. Ethel Applebee took the first step, in writing detailed letters home, but her mother Mabel saved Ethel's letters, her children preserved them, and her daughter Eleanor dedicated two years toward collecting more pieces and making sense of the sketches of a long-ago situation in a far-away location. We must be grateful to each of these generations.

Through Ethel Applebee's letters shine the flavor, frustrations, and triumphs of a young schoolteacher in a distant setting. Her dreams and experiences can be appreciated by women today, just as teachers would still agree that "about all you can do is be firm, and keep a twinkle in your eye." Through Ethel's letters we view households in early 20th century Maine and Kentucky.

We empathize with the disasters, joys, and disappointments of the Leightons and the Applebees, and accompany them through preparations for a home wedding. We glimpse race relations, in the North and the South. We learn about clothing, social life, and holiday celebrations, and we sense how Ethel is transforming her parental guidance and schooling into the mature, directed, socially-conscious, and loving adult her family cherished. And Ethel left a bonus— beautifully written poems which illustrate her commentary on certain situations.

I cannot imagine anyone who permits themselves to relax and absorb this account not to be moved, delighted, and inspired—moved by a daughter's recapture of a pivotal time in her mother's youth, delighted by the subject matter and photographs, and inspired to preserve a piece of our own personal history. For we and our loved ones will live on so long as we are remembered.

Eileen McGuckian
Rockville, Maryland

ACKNOWLEDGMENTS

One cannot come to the culmination of a writing task like this without realizing there were many people who contributed to its completion and publication. Editors were: Dr. Floyd T. Cunningham, Dean of the Asia-Pacific Nazarene Theological Seminary, Manila, Philippines, Denise Folwell, Leader of the Senior Writers Group, Gaithersburg, Maryland, and Eileen McGuckian, Executive Director of Peerless Rockville Historic Preservation, Ltd., Rockville, Maryland. Additional editorial assistance came from my daughter, Janice Leaman, and my sister, Jean Testerman.

Encouragement came from many relatives and friends: My children, Floyd T. Cunningham, Janice Leaman, and Diane Leclerc. My sisters, Alice Schmidt and Jean Testerman, and brother, Howard Leighton. My cousins from the Applebee and Leighton clans were very enthusiastic about the story of their "Aunt Ethel." They are: Jerry and Donna Applebee, Melburne and Jean Applebee, Muriel Applebee deBonaventura, Vinal and Marylin Applebee, Sylvia Applebee Lyon; Sally Dunham, daughter of Sara Leighton Aikins, Wilfred and Lucille Leighton, and Mary Striker, daughter of Ethel Leighton Ricker. My last living uncle, Philip Leighton (now deceased) and his wife, Bette, read parts of the story and liked it.

Also, my Gaithersburg Senior Center Writers Group leader, Judy Fitzwater; and members of my 2001 Group, Wilma Brady, Enchin Chen, Louise Diver, Elizabeth Engel, Paulette Geer, Joanne Johansen,

Ruth Law, Trish Mayyasi, Kim Nuyen, Peggy Kelly, Dorothy Trado and Lois Vallin who heard me read many of the chapters.

My research took me to Maine in 1998 and 2001 where I met Elizabeth Ellis of the Sebec, Maine, Historical Society. She showed me the site of the school where my mother taught in Sebec Village, Maine, and found documentary proof of my mother teaching there. Susan B. Eastman, Joanna Wilhelm and Nancy Wasson, Enterprise reporter, made it possible for me to visit my mother's home in Bucksport, Maine. Cousin Vinal Applebee took us to historical sites in Enfield, Maine, and Moosehead Lake, Maine, and Betty Corey showed us where my mother lived and taught in Easton, Maine. Dwight Fuller, last surviving student of Ethel Applebee, and his daughter, Sally Fuller, of Gaithersburg, Maryland have had great interest in the book throughout. I also received numerous materials, photographs and help from the Moosehead Historical Society, Greenville, Maine, from the Public Library of Lexington, Kentucky, and from the Amistad Research Center, Tulane University, New Orleans, Louisiana. Gordon B. McKinney, Director of the Appalachian Center, Berea College, boosted my morale when he read the complete manuscript and wrote, "I could not put it down." My friend, Bertha Smith, a former teacher, listened for many hours to my reading and insisted that the book should be published.

Last, I am grateful for the ongoing moral support of my friend, Eileen McGuckian, who would not allow me to lay the book aside, but from the beginning believed that it ought to be published. I thank her for her confidence in the story, her belief in me as a writer, and the expertise she shared in both editing and in assisting with the preparation of the manuscript for publication.

To all of you, and to others I may have forgotten, my sincere heartfelt thanks.

Eleanor W. Cunningham

CONTENTS

HISTORICAL BACKGROUND

Many years ago, my mother, Ethel Valentine Applebee, tucked away some old letters from her youth into a small cedar chest. At her death this cedar chest passed on to me. In 1997, I rediscovered the chest and read the letters.

Within the yellowed pages I was to meet a courageous young school teacher from Maine who, with great daring and spirit, embarked on an adventurous journey to Lexington, Kentucky. Here she was to teach at Chandler Normal School, a school for African American children.

Ethel was born in Enfield, Maine, on February 12, 1893, the daughter of Charles D. and Mabel B. Applebee. She had four brothers: Clarence, Sylvan, Vinal and Francis. When she was 13 years old her family moved to Bucksport, Maine, where Ethel enrolled in East Maine Conference Seminary and Normal School. On June 14, 1911, at age 18, she graduated with a teacher's diploma in hand and went on to teach in several Maine elementary schools. She received her teaching certificate from the Maine Department of Education on August 1, 1914.

The letters I found reflected how different her Northern culture was from that of the South, and the typical language of her day. My mother was fond of the Black students and teachers with whom she associated at Chandler Normal School. The usage of the words Negro and Colored was accepted in those times.[1]

Reading these letters aroused my curiosity. What took my mother from Maine, where she was born and reared, to Kentucky? Was it the warmer climate? Was it the spirit of adventure that spurred her, together with other female teachers of that era, to step out of the familiar accepted roles for women and do something different with her life? Or was it an inner impulse to aid a worthy cause, in this case, the education of the Black children of the South? Perhaps it was all of these.

My research suggested another possible reason for Ethel's going to teach in Kentucky. It was a promise she had made to a dear friend and cousin, Wellington Applebee Hodgkins. This young man, Ethel's age and also a teacher, planned to go South under the American Missionary Association to teach, but tuberculosis took his life at age 21. In a moving conversation with Wellington, Ethel learned of his dream, and she decided, if at all possible, to go in his place.

But behind the personal life of Ethel Applebee, I believed there was another story that needed to be told. Ethel was living toward the end of an era when missionary societies of several denominations, particularly the Methodist Episcopal and the Congregational churches, took it as their God-given task before, during and after the Civil War, to send teachers from the North to the South to establish schools and educate Black children. The American Missionary Association, an independent, non-sectarian organization, was foremost in this movement. Begun in 1846 under the leadership of such anti-slavery greats as Simeon S. Jocelyn, Arthur Tappan, and George

Whipple, the AMA sent literally thousands of teachers, men and women, to the South over the next eighty years.

Fortunately for young women like Ethel, and contributing to the education of children and grandchildren of slaves, another national trend addressed the demand for skilled teachers. In the early 1800s "normal schools," teacher training institutions, were established, following a pattern begun in France, Germany and Great Britain. (The first normal school in the United States was started in Lexington, Massachusetts in 1839.) In addition to the required ten years of public education, they offered a two-year training course that produced thousands of teachers, many only eighteen or nineteen years old. The movement to send teachers into the South caught on with many young women from New England as well as from New York, Ohio, Michigan, and Illinois. Because so many young men had been killed in the Civil War, they had given up hope of marriage. Now, when the demand was so great, trained teachers were ready to fill that need. "Scholars estimate that one in every five women in Massachusetts taught school at least once in her lifetime by the middle of the century. By the end of the century education was a largely female domain and a feminine mission."[2]

The American Missionary Association often solicited funds from philanthropists in order to build private schools, promising to name a school for the donor. Mrs. Phoebe Chandler of Boston donated $15,000 to build a school in Lexington, Kentucky, to prepare Black students to teach, and the AMA gave it her name.[3] Chandler Normal School opened in 1889. Thirty-one years later, in 1920, two Maine teachers, Lena Spencer, and my mother, Ethel Valentine Applebee, caught up in the wave of teachers headed South, were appointed to Chandler Normal School. Sara Leighton had gone the year before. All three of them had been trained in a Maine normal school.

These three young teachers were to find that the cultural climate of Kentucky was far different from that of Maine. They would not be accepted by the white community there, and they would also experience hostility from the parents of most of their students, even though they came as well-intentioned teacher/missionaries.

Also significant was the formidable debate going on in the South at that time between Black leaders who held that industrial training was more advantageous for the Black children of the South, and those who supported a liberal arts education. Booker T. Washington became a-well known spokesman for industrial education, while W. E. B. Du Bois espoused the need of the Black race for a liberal arts education. The American Missionary Association fostered both.[4]

Many Black leaders found industrial education appealing, partly because philanthropy subsidized it, and even more, because it fitted the moral-economic ideology of advancement that was in the ascendency.[5]

Booker T. Washington of Tuskegee, who exercised great influence throughout the South and among government leaders, advocated industrial education as the key to Black progress.[6]

It was natural, then, that many Southern educators resented the intrusion of the Northern teachers, who, bound together by their vision of a "redeemed South," attempted to accomplish their goals by bringing the virtues esteemed by mid-nineteenth century Americans as taught in nearly every school and from every pulpit. These included industry, frugality, honesty, sobriety, marital fidelity, self-reliance, self-control, godliness and love of country. "Their zeal proposed to establish beachheads of Christian piety and Yankee know-how in the moral wilderness of the defeated Confederacy. Some dreamed of the day when enough teachers could be supplied to make a New England of the whole South."[7]

Some Southern educators viewed this attitude as arrogance. They believed their Black children were being deprived of their cultural heritage. They wanted to build upon their own culture, using their own abilities, strengths, beliefs, religion, skills, trades, and intellect. They did not need these "pious, strange looking, strange-talking stiff and formal ladies and gentlemen of the far off North to tell them how to do that. Adding to the cultural barrier was the language the Northerners spoke, with its "foreign" accent; it was difficult to make sense out of what they were saying."[8]

Nevertheless, W. E. B. Du Bois reminded Washington that "many of the teachers of the industrial and elementary schools had attended liberal arts institutions and that until many more did so, Black leadership and the Negro race would be seriously retarded."[9]

As can be seen from a brief description of its colleges, the American Missionary Association did not advocate a particular type of education to the exclusion of others. That the Association found industrial training and liberal arts compatible was not surprising. Both were popular in mid-nineteenth century America.[10] Whether Ethel was aware of the "head versus hands" debate in the South is unknown, but since she had received a liberal arts education in Maine, that was her assignment at Chandler. On the other hand, Sara Leighton, a graduate of Farmington State Normal School, Farmington, Maine, was sent to Chandler to teacher home economics and related industrial subjects.

These teachers were motivated to go South by a genuine desire to assist Blacks, and most loved their work among them. Many considered it a calling. As a group they were far more sympathetic to Blacks than was the country at large at that time. Scores of teachers taught without pay, "asking no reward but the pleasure of being allowed to do the work."[11]

C. M. Shackford, of Mississippi, one of the early teachers sent out by the American Missionary Association, wrote, "Ours is a truly missionary work. In our isolation from society, in teaching the ignorant, in deprivation of many comforts, and in being the scorn and derision of the community, there is a glory, an excellence, and a satisfaction in the work."[12]

While there are thousands of hand-written letters and reports by these American Missionary Association teachers held in the archives at Armistad Research Center, Tulane University, New Orleans, McKeldin Library at the University of Maryland and other universities, I could find published accounts of only two other AMA teachers. One was Sara Jane Foster, a shoemaker's daughter from Gray, Maine, and the other Marion Stone from the Berkshires of Massachusetts. With this dearth of published personal stories by or about AMA teachers, I felt the personal story of Ethel Valentine Applebee would be a significant contribution to the history of these thousands of often unheralded teachers.

The information in the letters and my mother's decision to accept the challenge to teach at Chandler in Kentucky made me realize I had stumbled onto a story that needed to be placed in the historical context of the larger story—that of the tremendous impact the AMA had on educating the children of the South during and after Reconstruction. So here is the true story of "Miss Apple," another brave young Maine school teacher. As necessary I used my imagination to enhance the events, filling in the blanks by adding details and conversation as they might have happened.

Chandler Normal School was unlike the small one-or two-room schools of Maine. A three-story brick building with an auditorium seating 500, it enjoyed a fine reputation and supplied many of the teachers for the public schools. Author John D. Wright, Jr. recorded, "One of the major advances for black education in Lexington was the establishment of the Chandler Normal School to meet the demand for black teachers."[13]   F. J. Webster, principal of Chandler Normal School in 1898, wrote: "For the excellent work done in the Colored city schools, the American Missionary Association is largely responsible. Its educational institutions were the models after which the city schools were patterned."[14] Another author, George C. Wright, writes, "Established in 1889, Chandler enjoyed solid financial backing. As a result, the school existed for four decades and offered a wide range of courses, all of which, according to one survey, were well done."[15]

Besides the usual teacher training curriculum, Chandler offered industrial subjects such as home economics, sewing, cooking, and the trades.

Ethel would probably have stayed at Chandler School for another year but for a turn of events that was to change her life forever. Sara Leighton, the Chandler teacher from Cumberland Center, Maine, invited Ethel to come home with her for a visit at the end of the school year, 1921. Ethel accepted the invitation and met Sara's brother, Howard. It was love at first sight for both Howard and Ethel. They became engaged, and Ethel gave up her teaching career at Chandler.

Howard and Ethel's romance is described in the second set of letters that I discovered, buried beneath the first set in the little cedar chest. These were love letters Howard and Ethel wrote to each other between September 26 and October 14, 1921. Howard wrote from the Leighton farm in Cumberland Center, Maine; Ethel wrote from her home in Bucksport, 150 miles away. There at her home on October 20, 1921, they exchanged wedding vows.

In reading her letters I came to know her as a young person. Her daring and spirit evoked my admiration. Years later as her daughter I was required to study hard, strive for excellence, be honest, and do the chores assigned to me. I recall fondly her "school marm" mannerisms and the "twinkle in her eye," her New England fortitude, and her heart for children.

Eventually Howard and Ethel left their families and their first home in Falmouth, and moved to Rockville, Maryland in 1923, where Howard had accepted a job with Rock Creek Nursery. Ethel missed her beloved Maine and her family, but made new friends as she became involved as a Sunday School teacher in the little church that held services in the two-room Montrose School up the road. She served as President of the school PTA and was a substitute teacher there. Ethel and Howard had four children—Alice, Jean, Howard and myself. Ethel passed on her love of teaching to Alice and Jean, who became public school teachers.

Howard died of a heart attack in Rockville, January 20, 1950, at age 55, and Ethel died in a nursing home in Olney, Maryland, November 15, 1973, at age 80. She was buried beside her husband at Arlington National Cemetery, Washington, D.C.

Eleanor W. Cunningham

**Ethel Valentine Applebee, age 18,
Bucksport, Maine.
EVA Collection**

Chapter One - A Dream and a Promise

On a June morning in 1920, a young, attractive school teacher by the name of Ethel Valentine Applebee was traveling south by train from Easton, Maine, to her home in Bucksport. There she had lived with her parents and four brothers until a teaching position had taken her elsewhere.

As the train chugged its way through the deep forest, Ethel leaned her head back on the seat cushion behind her and closed her eyes. "Here I am, headed home, after only three years. I feel like I am taking another daring leap in the dark." Yes, the northern winters had been extremely cold, and there wasn't much excitement for a girl who loved excitement. But in her pocket was the main reason for her returning to Bucksport at that time. It was a letter from Lena Spencer, her longtime friend since grammar school days in Enfield. That letter would change both their lives dramatically in the days ahead.

Lena's letter had been providential. The letter arrived in April, the day after Ethel had gone to a special meeting at the Easton Methodist church to hear a speaker tell about opportunities for teachers in the South. They would teach in private schools for Negro children, training them to become teachers of their own race. The speaker really caught Ethel's attention when he told of the many New England young ladies who had already gone. He said the door was wide open for other teachers to go; all they needed to do was apply to the American Missionary Association!

A deep restlessness had settled over Ethel's spirit after hearing that speaker; she didn't know why. It was a longing that she could not define. What would it be like to be one of those single ladies going off to do missionary work in the South? Was that the challenge for which she was looking? Might this provide the purpose she needed to quiet the restlessness within her? Oh, to do something magnificent with one's life, something glorious and meaningful! She recalled the title of a little book her mother had given her, *The Beauty of a Life of Service*, by Phillips Brooks, the renowned clergyman. She remembered some of the words: "It is not for the salvation of your life, it is not for the salvation of yourself... It is that you may take your place in the great army of God and go forward having something to do with the work that He is doing in the world."[1] A life of service, doing God's work, she mused. Yes, that would give her peace.

Ethel knew that the letter in her pocket from Lena was not the only reason she was traveling South from Easton that June day of 1920. The other reason was a personal one that she had never shared with anyone. It had to do with her cousin, "Wellie."

Wellington A. Hodgkins was also a close friend. He had been a student at East Maine Conference Seminary, and active in sports, playing on the school baseball team his senior year.

Students, 1911, East Maine Conference Seminary, Bucksport, Maine.
Ethel V. Applebee, first row, fifth from the left.
EVA Collection

Wellington A. Hodgkins, Cousin of Ethel Applebee.
EVA Collection

A quiet, studious young man, intellectual, given to much reading, Wellie was a favorite among the students and the people of Bucksport. He and Ethel often met in the school library to talk. Valedictorian of the 1913 class, like Ethel, he wanted to be a teacher. Though he had been in ill health for three years, he applied for and was appointed to a teaching position in Lowell, Maine, near Enfield. However, as his health worsened, he was forced to return to his home in Bucksport at the end of the fall term.

Ethel recalled that fateful evening in late December when Wellington knocked at the door of her home. He was so pale, so emaciated, and his voice so weak. "Hi, Ethel. I'm home," he said with a faint smile. "May I come in?"

"Of course, Wellie. How nice to see you." She led him into the sitting room where he sat on the horsehair couch facing the bay window that overlooked the street. The setting sun was casting long shadows over the peaceful Penobscot River below. She sat beside him, disturbed by the obvious deterioration of his health since she last saw him.

"How was teaching in Lowell? Do you plan to return next term?" she asked, all the while knowing that he surely would not be able to go back to teaching.

"No, Ethel, I'm afraid not. I have been to see my doctor and it is just as I feared. I have tuberculosis. He hopes that complete rest will bring me through it, but there's no guarantee that I will ever be well."

"I'm so sorry, Wellie. Truly I am." Tears sprang to her eyes as she reached out her hand and placed it on his. He was grateful for her

4

comforting presence and concern. Tuberculosis, the "white plague," had taken so many among them.

"Ethel, I may not live long. I'm only 21 years old, and I'm afraid I'll never see my dream come true. I guess I never told you that I had hoped one day to accept an appointment to teach in the South. Some of my friends have gone, and they love the work. I enjoy teaching, and I adore children, and that would be such a great opportunity to show the love of Christ to a very needy people." He paused and sighed deeply. "Maybe someone else can go in my place."

Ethel was sobered, and spoke again, "Did the doctor say how long… how long… you have?"

"He says I'm in the last stages. I only have months to live, Ethel."

"Oh, Wellie, I am so sorry. We've been such good friends." She paused, "Wellie, are you ready…to die?"

"Ethel, you are one of my dearest friends, and I know I can speak frankly to you. I have asked myself that question many times. I have searched my heart, and I have the assurance that all is right between God and me. Do you remember, Ethel, when we were children, and we attended the little church in Enfield? Do you remember the time a visiting evangelist came to hold a revival meeting and several went forward to accept Christ? I went up, and as I remember, you did too. I can still remember the clean feeling I had, knowing that Christ had forgiven my sins and taken them away."

Ethel replied softly, "Yes, I remember that day."

Wellie continued. "I have endeavored from that day forward to live the way I believe the Lord would have me live. Yes, Ethel, I believe I am ready to die, if God should call me home."

Tears were streaming down Ethel's face. She tightened her grip on her friend's hand and they sat quietly. The sun had set, and darkness crept into the room.

Ethel rose and lit the kerosene lamp and a soft light touched Wellie's face, enhancing a look of sweet peace she had never seen there before. As she did so she thought of the dream he had shared, the dream of going South to teach.

"Wellie," she asked, sitting down beside him again. "Tell me more about your dream. How does a person get appointed to teach in the South? I think I know of someone who might be interested in going in your place."

Often in the following months and years Ethel wondered how her promise would be realized. Then Lena's letter arrived.

When Ethel was only thirteen, at her mother's insistence the Applebee family had moved from Enfield, her birthplace, to Bucksport so that Ethel, second eldest child in the family, could enroll at East Maine Conference Seminary and become a teacher. Ethel's mother, Mabel, had been a teacher. (Father had chosen to stay in Enfield to work the farm for at least part of the year.) East Maine Conference Seminary, located just blocks from their home, offered a two-year teacher training course. Ethel recalled the day she graduated, June 14, 1911. She was the valedictorian. Some of the words of her speech came back to her:

"It gives us joy when we think of the difficulties we have conquered and the mysterious future spreading before us in which, with youthful hope and optimism, we see only the brightness, the opportunity to surmount obstacles, and to make our niche in the wonderful building of life." Her closing remarks had been: "If we cannot all reach the highest to which some have aspired, we may do our best from day to day..."[2]

At age eighteen Ethel graduated from the Seminary's Normal School, a teacher's diploma in hand, hoping she would get an appointment soon.

**Mt. Kineo House, 1910, Moosehead Lake, Maine.
Courtesy Moosehead Historical Society**

Bored with the train ride, Ethel's mind drifted back to the summer of 1911, when she worked as a waitress at Mt. Kineo House at Moosehead Lake. Moosehead was the largest lake in Maine, forty miles long and ten miles wide. Mt. Kineo House was situated on a large peninsula.

A favorite resort for the well-to-do of that day, it had been rebuilt in 1910. Its crowning glory was the new dining room, nearly 200 feet long, surrounded by great windows through which one could see the shining blue lake, the green forests, and distant blue peaks. Behind it rose Mt. Kineo (Indian name for "flint"), with its 700 foot solid flint stone cliff, imposing and majestic, from which it was said that Indians obtained flint for their arrow heads.

Main Dining Room, Mt. Kineo House, Moosehead Lake, Maine 1920. EVA Collection

Moosehead Lake Steamer landing tourists at new Mt. Kineo House 1920.
Courtesy Moosehead Historical Society

This new 500-room Mt. Kineo House was heated throughout by steam, and used water from a spring which was declared by the Science Department of Bowdoin College to be one of the finest drinking waters in the world. It boasted such services as telegraph, telephone and stock market reports, and for the benefit of its guests had a fine library, music room, writing rooms, smoking rooms and play rooms for children.

It was while there that Ethel received her first offer of a teaching position. It was an invitation from Rev. E. S. Burrill, School Superintendent, for Ethel to teach at little Sebec Village, near Milo, for ten weeks that fall. His letter, dated August 7, 1911, read:

> *Miss Ethel Applebee*
>
> *Mt. Kineo House*
>
> *Kineo, Me.*
>
> *Dear Miss Applebee:*
>
> *Your letter applying for a school was received, and now I will reply. We have a vacancy. District No. 11, a school of nine scholars, wages $8 per week for which we want a teacher. The term will be ten weeks, probably.*
>
> *Would you like to take this school? If so, please let me hear from you at once. A little later we shall appoint a day for the teachers to meet and take the required examination. Of this we will let you know, should you choose to come.*
>
> *We expect our schools will open Tuesday, Sept. 5, possibly not until the Monday following.*
>
> *I am enclosing stamped and self-addressed envelope.*
>
> *Hope to have an early reply. I am*
>
> *Cordially yours*
>
> *(Rev.) E. S. Burrill, Supt.*[3]

Ethel replied immediately, accepting the invitation. She left Mt. Kineo House for Sebec on September first, boarding the train on the Greenville Branch of the Bangor and Piscataquis Railroad. The Sebec station was situated near the one-room school where she would teach.[4] Mr. and Mrs. Fred Bumpus, a couple well past their sixties, met her in their carriage; she would be boarding with them for the term. He was tall with thinning gray hair, she was short and plump with a dimple in her chin. They were warm and hospitable, seeming to understand that she was a bit nervous about her new assignment. They told her they had boarded several previous teachers.

The school was only a half mile from the house, and after unpacking her belongings, Ethel walked down the dirt road to the one-room school to inspect her classroom. She was surprised that Rev. Burrill, the school superintendent, was there, no doubt making sure the school was ready for the new teacher on opening day. He was a distinguished looking middle-aged man in black suit and tie. A gold watch chain hung from his pocket.

He greeted Ethel pleasantly, and stopped to talk. He told Ethel there were nine such schools in Sebec as it was the policy of the township school board that no child should walk more than two miles to school. Ethel observed the usual two entrances, one for the boys and one for the girls, and the two privies attached to the rear of the building. A large blackboard hung on the rear wall, and this is where Ethel envisioned seating the children for their graded arithmetic lessons.

Superintendent Burrill explained that Ethel was to teach reading, grammar, history, physiology, geography, penmanship, and writing in addition to mathematics.[5] Seminary courses familiarized her with these subjects; she felt certain they were within her capabilities.

Superintendent Burrill informed Ethel that she was also to lead the children in reciting the Lord's Prayer at the beginning of the school day, as well as the Flag Salute and a Bible reading. She was to have

Letter of Supt. of Schools E. S. Burrill, Sebec village, Maine August 7, 1911, to Ethel V. Applebee at Mt. Kineo House, Kineo, Maine.
EVA Collection

Harriman School Museum, Sebec Village, Maine.
Courtesy Sebec Historical Society

nine pupils, ranging from six to twelve years old, and she looked forward to meeting them. A cold winter would mean a constant watch to keep the wood stove burning, and someone to keep the wood box full. Thankfully, there was no shortage of wood in Maine, and Ethel would assign the older boys to that task.[6]

A large hand bell sat on the teacher's desk at the front of the room. Ethel was to ring the bell at 9:00 a.m. for school to begin, and again at 3:00 p.m. for dismissal. The children would bring their lunch pails from home. After Superintendent Burrill left the building, Ethel found a piece of chalk and proudly wrote "Miss Applebee" on the blackboard. She took a seat at the teacher's desk, collecting her thoughts for the coming school day.

Even though the term was short, Ethel enjoyed teaching that fall in Sebec Village. The children were bright and learned quickly. One of their favorite activities was the spelling bee for which, at the end of each day, they lined up in front of Miss Applebee's desk. Merits were awarded on Friday to those who had a perfect score for the week. It was obvious they enjoyed school and liked their teacher.

The experience at Sebec Village gave Ethel the confidence that she could succeed as a teacher, and she was determined to be a good one. With that confidence and what was left of her $80 earnings, Ethel was returning now to Bucksport to look for another teaching position.

Interior of Harriman School Museum, 1998.
Author's Collection

Ethel loved Bucksport, and she had many friends there, including some who were still in the Seminary. But she needed money, and since it did not appear that she would be getting a teaching position soon, she looked for other work. She worked for a while for a couple who ran a small hotel, and when the hotel closed and the owner died, she continued to work for his wife, Mrs. Rice, who was in need of a housekeeper and companion.

But Ethel's heart was set on teaching. This was her calling. She continued to send out applications to several school superintendents, and applied to Aroostook County, the most northern county in Maine.

Ethel was delighted when a letter finally came in late August, 1917, Mr. Glover, the Superintendent of Schools at Fort Fairfield in Aroostook County wrote that Ethel was being appointed for a two-year term at the one-room Fuller School in Easton, Maine. Her room and board would be provided, and salary was $14 a week. The school would open on October 1.

Ethel wrote her acceptance immediately. She guessed there weren't a lot of applications for a teaching position so far north, just one mile from the Canadian border. Northern Maine was noted for its cold winters; she had heard that temperatures could get as low as 30 below, and snow lay deep on the ground all winter. Ethel was thrilled at the prospect of an adventure in far-off Aroostook County. People called it "The County," which covered an area larger than Connecticut and Rhode Island combined. It was mostly wilderness and trees, waterways and potato farms, but there were children to teach there, and so Ethel would go.

During the summer, before leaving for Easton, she and her Mother bought yards of material, sewing the warmer clothing she would need. She also packed her high black leather boots, warm red mittens with matching woolen scarf and hat, which her mother had knit for her and given her for Christmas the year before. Her new black woolen coat reached to her ankles. She planned to buy a pair of snowshoes in Easton at the Indian Exchange before the heavy snows came. She took time that July to write her lesson plans.

She had taken the train going north on that Friday morning in late September, 1917. As she stepped off the train in late evening she could feel the chill of fall. Walter and Lillian Fuller met her at the train station in Easton with their carriage. Walter was a tall, quiet man of about fifty. As he took the reins to drive the horses, Ethel noticed the large calloused hands of a potato farmer. Lillian wore horn rimmed glasses, and her hair was pulled back tightly in a bun. She had a warm, friendly smile. They took her to their country home on Fuller Road, where she was to board for the next two years.

The Fuller family was good to her. Theirs was a huge house, even by Maine standards, with its two floors, sixteen rooms, three large hallways, attic, and basement. On a forty-acre potato farm, it had been built by Grandfather Fuller with the idea that two families would live there. He and Grandmother lived on one side, and Walter and Lillian and their several children lived on the other. Ethel was given a large comfortable second-floor corner room overlooking the front. The

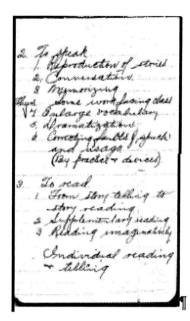

Ethel V. Applebee's Lesson Plans, July 1917.
EVA Collection

Winton Car owned by the Fuller family, Easton, Maine, ca. 1917
Courtesy Walter Corey

room contained a high black poster bed, oak desk and chair, small cane rocker, wide closet and colorful hand-made braided rug. It was all she needed.

Walter and Lillian Fuller as well as their children made Ethel feel welcome. They were hard working people, and frugal. They invited Ethel to accompany them each Sunday to the Easton Methodist Church, all of them piling into their large Winton touring car. (She was told it was only one of three in the entire county!)[7]

At first Ethel was homesick for Bucksport, and especially for her mother. But gradually she became a part of this loving family. It was like home in the fall evenings when they all gathered around the large pine kitchen table for supper.

The Fuller boys, Vernon, Cecil, Darrell, Ben, and little eight year old Dwight (who was to be one of her pupils), reminded her of her own four brothers, Clarence, Sylvan, Vinal, and Francis, with whom she had often played school. Perhaps that was one reason teaching came naturally to her. (Clarence, her oldest brother, had been drafted into the U.S. Army[8] after she left home to teach in Easton.)

Miraculously, it seemed to Ethel that day, things were falling into place. There had been the opportunity to hear about the American Missionary Association at the Methodist Church, and how to apply to be appointed to a school in the South. And then the letter from Lena. Now, on her way to Bucksport, Ethel knew in her heart she was about to embark on the adventure that would fulfill the promise made to Wellington years before. Her heart leaped at the prospect.

Fuller Family with whom Ethel Applebee stayed while teaching in Easton, Maine. Dwight, 8, in front, was one of her pupils.
EVA Collection

Chapter Two - Bangor, Bucksport, and Beyond

To while away the hours on the train, Ethel thought again of those first days of her appointment at Fuller School. She had been so eager to see the schoolhouse.

After breakfast she asked Mrs. Fuller, "Do you suppose I could see my classroom this morning?" Mrs. Fuller smiled and took a key from a hook behind the kitchen door. She handed it to Ethel. "Of course. I'll have Vernon drive you down in the carriage."

As Ethel turned the key in the rusty lock and pushed open the creaking door, the musty smell from the school, unventilated all summer, greeted her. She opened windows to let in the fresh air, which already carried a chilling hint of winter. She counted the desks. Eight rows of six each made forty-eight. Even though she was an experienced teacher, that would be quite a handful, she thought. Teaching grades one through eight would keep her on her toes, a daunting challenge for even the best of teachers!

Ethel browsed through the cupboards to locate supplies. She was happy to find several textbooks, though well worn.[9] Packages of paper had been stored in a low cupboard. Understandably, there were signs the mice had found it before she did. Next, she found a few broken pencils which lay in a box on her desk. She hoped the children brought their own pencils. No doubt they also brought their lunch pails from home.

Ethel was pleased to find large blackboards, one behind her desk and two on the opposite wall on each side of the door that led to the attached woodshed. As a Maine girl, she was well aware that keeping the wood box filled during the cold winter days would be a constant chore. The willing Fuller boys had assured her that they would keep the fires burning.

She looked for chalk and found only a few pieces in a box in her desk along with an eraser. Taking out a piece, she carefully wrote in her well-formed Palmer script on the front blackboard, "My name is Miss Applebee."

The school drinking water, Ethel was told, came from a well at the house next to the school. It would be a short walk each day for one of the larger children to fill the bucket which sat inside the door. Outside, the playground was overgrown with weeds. However, the building seemed to be in good repair. She made a note to see if she could find the flag that was to fly from the pole in front of the building.

With little time to waste, Ethel worked each day at the school, preparing lessons, cleaning, dusting, and arranging the desks as she liked them. The day before school opened, a little girl and her mother stopped in, bringing the flag. They had taken it home over the summer to wash so that it would be crisp and clean for the start of the year. Smiling, Ethel had the feeling they came also to look over the new teacher. They were from the Ames family that lived next door, and she would have little Margaret in the second grade. She had already met another prospective student soon after her arrival, seven-year-old Vera Louise Johnston, who lived just across the street from the Fullers.

School opened the first day in October. (Mr. Fuller explained to Ethel that school opened late in Aroostook County because children were needed to help harvest the potato crop.) That first day the students arrived on time and stood hesitantly around the front of the building. They were waiting to see their new teacher, wondering, no doubt, if she would be strict or easy. She had them line up in front of the doorstep, younger children first, older children in the rear.

As they marched in she directed them to their seats. They soon learned Miss Applebee meant to have an orderly classroom. Ethel was determined to keep the upper hand and leave no doubt as to who was in charge. She gave the older boys manual tasks to do to make them feel necessary to the success of the school, sweeping the floor, and washing the blackboards. She asked the older girls to help the younger children with their lessons while she was teaching other grades. Mrs. Fuller had told Ethel before she left for school on that first morning that if Dwight gave her any trouble at all, just let her know and she would "take care of him." Dwight knew that, and was a model pupil, learning his lessons well and helping this pretty teacher who had come to live in his home.[10]

As the Bangor and Aroostook train chugged along over the miles, Ethel's mind went back to that unforgettable freezing January day in Easton when she had started for school. The heavy snow had fallen steadily throughout the night, and the wind had blown huge drifts across the roads and fields. Fuller School seldom closed because of the weather, and she vowed it wouldn't close that day. Ethel pulled her boots on over two pair of woolen stockings, put on two pairs of mittens, tied her wool scarf tightly about her neck, pulled her woolen cap well down over her ears, and bravely set off in her snow shoes across snow-covered fields. She covered her face the best she could and navigated by watching the tops of the fence posts, nearly hidden in the snow drifts.

Ethel Applebee in snowshoes in front of Fuller home.
EVA Collection

Though the wind had died down somewhat, it was bitterly cold. The Fullers had told her to beware of frostbite; it could happen before she realized it. By the time she arrived at school, her right cheek was numb and the skin had turned blue. She feared it was frostbitten, so she rubbed snow on it until the feeling returned. In a few minutes Kenneth Powers and Fred Henderson, eighth graders, arrived. Seeing how chilled their teacher was, they quickly built the fire.

That was the day when she decided she would try for another school next year, farther South, where the winters were not so frigid. In fact, during the winter of her second year in Easton she had moved to the Ames home next to the school to avoid walking the half—mile through snowdrifts in winter.

* * * * * * * * * * *

The train was moving slowly, stopping occasionally at small towns to allow a passenger or two to get on or off. First there was Bridgewater, then Houlton, the county seat, Oakfield, Sherman Mills, and then Lincoln. Obviously this was a mill town, for there were piles of logs waiting beside the tracks to be processed into paper pulp at the mill operated by Lincoln Pulp and Paper Company. The air smelled strongly of sulphur, used in the process of breaking down the wood into pulp. It was not a pleasant odor; she guessed the people in that town, dependent upon the paper industry, just got used to it.

It was past noon when Ethel remembered the basket lunch Mrs. Fuller had given her. Opening it, she found homemade biscuits and cheese, two hard-boiled eggs and a piece of Mrs. Fuller's delicious spice cake. She had filled her thermos too; the hot tea was refreshing.

More miles of nothing but trees. No wonder they called this the "Pine Tree State," thought Ethel. Patches of snow under the trees reminded Ethel how short the Maine summers were—just July and August, and then winter comes fast on the heels of a chilling autumn. Ethel watched for glimpses of the beautiful Penobscot River that flows to Bucksport and beyond to the Atlantic Coast. It was like seeing an old friend, and there were lakes too. How many were there in Maine? No wonder the Southerners came here for vacations. Soon the rumbling of the train wheels indicated they were crossing the river bridge trestle, and then they were plunging, faster now, through that long lonely stretch of wilderness before reaching the town of Howland.

Birthplace of Ethel Valentine Applebee, Enfield, Maine, February 12, 1893.
Author's Collection

She was coming upon familiar territory now. Just east of Howland was West Enfield, and just beyond, Enfield, where she was born and reared. She caught a glimpse of the church steeple through the trees. Enfield was a small village with a few houses, a garage, a store, the Baptist Church, a school, and a family graveyard on the hill where most stones were marked "Applebee." Just outside of town was the family farm where she was born and had lived as a child.

Mabel B. and Charles D. Applebee, parents of Ethel V. Applebee, Enfield, Maine.
EVA Collection

**Baptist Church which Ethel attended while living in Enfield, Maine.
Author's Collection**

How often she had watched the train streaking by their lower meadow. Little did she dream then that one day she would ride that train North to Easton, and now South again.

Old Town was next, the site of the Penobscot Indian island reservation. Tourists came here to buy authentic Indian relics and souvenirs. Since long ago, when they were a part of the powerful Abnaki Nation, these Indians had built their superb quality canoes. They lived in small houses now; the wigwams were just for show. The Indians welcomed the vacationers who came in the summer, for they brought a little revenue to the struggling reservation. Ethel had a few of their souvenirs which she used in her classes—baskets, small canoes, bows and arrows, and an Indian doll.

After the train passed Orono, the University town, the next stop would be Bangor. She recalled her mother telling her that the first settler of Bangor was one of her ancestors on the Buzzell side of the family.[11] Bangor, gateway to the hunting and fishing industry in northern and eastern Maine, had been one of the great logging ports of the United States. Here Ethel would change trains for Bucksport. Though the total distance of the trip thus far was only one hundred fifty-five miles, it had taken almost seven hours because of local stops along the way. This railroad was one of the principal means of transportation between the larger cities of Maine, carrying not only passengers and mail, but also livestock, potatoes, and other farm produce to Maine markets, as well as to markets as far away as Boston.

Ethel gathered her things together. Soon it would be Bangor, then Bucksport, and beyond.

Chapter Three - Mt. Kineo and Kentucky

Over the years Ethel had often thought of Wellie and their conversation. Nothing had come of it until that letter came from Lena. She took the letter out of her pocket to read again. In it was the compelling reason she had turned her steps Southward:

"Dear Et, (Lena had always called her 'Et'). "Are you ready for a big adventure? How would you like to leave the cold North and go South where there is little snow and a lot of opportunity to make our mark in the world? You have probably heard that many Yankee girls have gone South to teach in private schools, and have made as much as $15 a week. I saw an advertisement in the Bucksport Enterprise yesterday about a Chandler Normal School in Lexington, Kentucky needing teachers from the North to teach Negro children. How does that sound, Et? Let me know if you are interested. I am, and I wish you would go with me. Please answer right away. We could apply now and be on our way for the term beginning in October. Love, Lena."

**Applebee home at 44 Broadway, Bucksport, Maine, early 1900s.
Author's Collection**

Lena was always the daring one, and this sounds just like her, thought Ethel, as she remembered the two of them had engaged in many childish escapades. They had separated after grammar school graduation in 1906, Ethel moving to Bucksport with her parents and brothers, while Lena went off to a different normal school. They had not been together for several years. Now Lena was to meet her at the train in Bucksport. They'd probably get a summer job together and then, perhaps, by fall be on their way to Kentucky to teach in that rich private school. It all sounded so exciting. Ethel could hardly wait to see her friend and to discuss their plans for the future. And, of course, to see her parents and her brothers again. Ethel also remembered her promise to dear Wellington, and was thrilled with the possibility that soon that promise would become a reality.

The train whistle signaled the next stop; the conductor called out, "Bangor, Bangor, all out for Bangor." As the train came to a jolting halt, Ethel hurriedly collected her things and jumped off. Here she transferred to the Maine Central train that would take her home.

Ethel loved Bucksport, once an international port renowned for shipbuilding, resting on the slopes above the blue Penobscot River. She loved the sturdy brick buildings of the seminary where she learned to be a teacher and made so many friends, and she loved the white frame building on Broadway, her home, one of four identical houses built by Joseph L. Buck in 1876 for his children. The Bucks were their next door neighbors.

The train followed the river and in forty-five minutes pulled into the Bucksport station. Ethel peered out of the dusty window for a glimpse of Lena. There she was! Tall, with curling brown hair and smiling as usual, Lena looked the same as Ethel remembered her. Ethel rushed to the door and jumped down. Lena threw her arms around her. "So good to see you, Et. How was your trip? Where's your trunk?"

Ethel, pointing to the porter who was just bringing her trunk to the platform, said, "How did you get here? Did Papa bring you? So good to see you, Lena." Her heart warmed and tears came to her eyes. How much she had missed this good friend; she was like a sister. Perhaps Lena was another reason why she left Easton.

Lena pointed across the street to a Model T Ford. "That's mine. Do you believe I can drive? We're traveling by car, Et!"

A porter toted the trunk to the car and placed it in the back. Ethel climbed in the high front seat and waited. Lena went to the front of the car, turned the hand crank several times. Finally the motor started. Lena jumped into the driver's seat. Ethel marveled at the dubious driving expertise of her friend! With some chugging and coughing the Model T took off, climbing the hill and turning down Broadway.

As they drove into the yard, Papa was pulling the loaded hay wagon into the barn. Ethel waved to him as she jumped out of the car, hurrying to greet Mother who had stepped out of the side door. Tall and stately, her dark hair pulled up in a knot on top of her head, she was very dear to Ethel and the one person she had missed most.

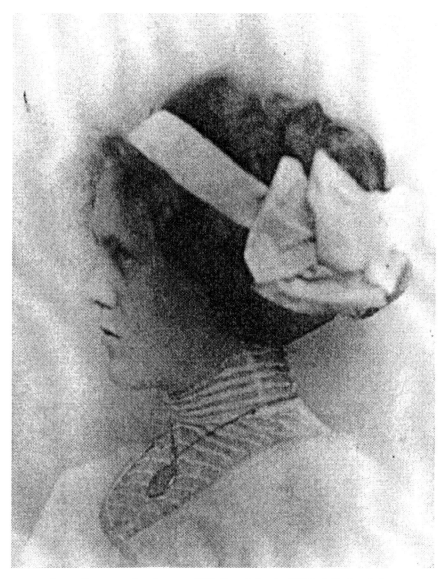

**Lena Spencer, teacher and lifetime friend of Ethel V. Applebee.
EVA Collection**

Mabel B. Applebee and daughter Ethel V. Applebee, early 1900s.
EVA Collection

Mabel Applebee had wanted the best for this only daughter of hers. Besides the twinkling, sometimes mischievous, blue eyes, the wavy auburn hair and attractive slender figure, Mabel had also seen in Ethel high ambition, unusual intelligence, wit and charm. Tears came to her eyes as Mabel saw her teacher-daughter jump from the car and run toward her. Ethel rushed to embrace her mother and felt the warmth of her familiar hug.

"Come in, come in. Supper is almost ready." Papa unloaded the trunk as he talked with Lena. Apple pies cooled on top of the wood stove, and Ethel savored the aroma of the baked beans and brown bread waiting in the oven. How good to be home!

That evening after the supper dishes were washed and dried, Ethel went to her room to unpack. In a few minutes Lena came in from the guest room next to Ethel's. The two friends talked long into the night, laughing and sharing their various teaching experiences of the past years.

Finally Ethel, sobering, said, "Now tell me about this Kentucky business. What did the ad say and when can we go?"

Lena, excited, replied, "You mean you really would go with me to teach in that school? Honest? Here, let me get the paper where I saw the advertisement."

"Teachers wanted," she read aloud, "Chandler Normal School, Lexington, Kentucky. Openings in primary, upper grades, and normal school. Salary $1,000 per year. Send resume and experience to Dr. James W. Cooper, Secretary, American Missionary Association, 53 John Street, New York, N.Y."[12]

"What do you think, Et? Shall we try it? It would be fun and we would be doing some good, too. Teaching Negro children—that would be something we have never done before."

"That's true, Lena. Do you think these are poor children, or perhaps, possibly, children of the upper class, it being a private school?"[13]

"I guess we'll find out. Maybe some of both. I am sure this school wants teachers who are not prejudiced against the Negro, and who would be willing to stick it out, no matter what. Let's do it!"

Ethel, still sober, replied, "It's going to take some money to get there, and new clothes, probably. It's not nearly as cold there as in northern Maine. But first we must send them a letter telling them how smart and how experienced we are!"

Lena laughed. "Well, we do have experience, and of course you are the smart one. I wonder how much money we'll need. Train fare, of course, and some extra."

Ethel was thoughtful. "They pay very well. $1,000 a year is a lot more than I was making at Fuller School."

Lena paused. "What do you think your Mother will say? Have you told her about this?"

Ethel smiled, "Well you know, Lena, we are twenty-one and then some, so we can do whatever we like. But I think Mother will approve. She is the idealistic type, you know. Always wanted me to amount to something. We'll be going as missionaries, I suppose, as well as teachers, and she'll like that. And Papa won't care."

"Tomorrow we'll write the letter. This is so exciting. But I think we'd better plan to work this summer. Maybe go up to Mt. Kineo House again and wait tables as we did before. Tips are good there."

So many things to think about. Easton seemed far away now. Ethel could hardly sleep with all that was tumbling around in her pretty head. A decent salary, a nice school, warmer climate, and Lena would be there. Oh, how wonderful it was all going to be!

The next morning Lena and Ethel awoke early, excited about their coming adventure. Another summer at beautiful Mt.Kineo House on Moosehead Lake, and then a teaching job in Kentucky. After breakfast they went to the parlor desk; each penned a letter to the American Missionary Association. They wrote of their earnest desire to help educate the Negro children of the South, and requested an application for teaching positions. Later they hiked down to the Post Office and deposited the letters, hoping for a quick reply.

They also addressed letters to Mt. Kineo House, asking for summer jobs as waitresses, and noting that they had worked there previous summers. A reply came the following week. Yes, Mt. Kineo House was hiring for the summer; could they come in two weeks? The restaurant would open officially for the season the following weekend, the first of July.

When Ethel's mother asked at the noon meal that day what their plans were for the summer, Ethel told her of their application to Mt. Kineo House.

"And after that, Ethel? What plans do you have for the fall? Have you applied for a teaching position here?" She hoped Ethel would come to live at home again and teach at a school close by. It had been lonely without her.

"We're planning to save our money this summer and then hope to go to Kentucky to teach at Chandler Normal School, a private school, in Lexington. We've sent a letter to the American Missionary Association. They're looking for Northern teachers. Nothing definite yet. We still have to be accepted. Just think Mother, your daughter could be a missionary!"

Mabel said nothing in reply. Kentucky… Why Kentucky? Sometimes she thought this girl of hers was a little too ambitious for her own good. That was so far away, really a foreign land. But she would not stand in her way if that was what she really wanted to do.

Lena drove her Model T Ford up to beautiful Mt. Kineo. A small ferry took them across the lake to the Mt. Kineo peninsula. It was even more beautiful than Ethel remembered. On arrival Ethel and Lena settled into their comfortable dormitory rooms overlooking the lake, and then met with the head matron for their assignments. She asked them about their previous summer experiences there, seemed pleased with the answers, and assigned them both as head waitresses.

Other young women from all parts of the state had come for summer work. It was from one of these that Ethel heard the story of the French Canadian who lost his life at the Big Spring logging drive in Jackman, a small town not far from Mt. Kineo. Somehow it affected Ethel deeply, and stayed with her for a long time. After she was married she would write the account for her own children to read. She titled it, "The Purchased Possession."

A crowd of people stood upon the bank of the river. It was the first day of the great spring drive. Above the dam the icy water was filled with floating logs which had been rolled down from the great piles upon the banks. River drivers armed with cantdogs rolled the snowy timber into the water while others carrying pick poles pushed and coaxed the logs from their inclination to stick into the bank or to crowd into a jam. Many months before, the lumbermen had gone to the great northern woods and purchased the standing timber. During the months of cold weather great crews of men working with saw and axe had felled the trees which in turn had been sluiced down the icy hills to be piled on the side of the

38

woods road. From there they had been hauled and re-piled on the river bank.

Upon each log had been cut the lumberman's seal that each might claim his own at the time of the separation when the logs should be drawn out of the water at the end of the long trip down the river.

Now that the spring days had come, snow was melting, the river was open. In haste river drivers were sent for, and equipped with cocked boots, heavy mackinaws, woolen stockings, mittens and caps, they were arriving to be part of this opening day of the spring drive.

At first there was laughter and excited talk, then a hush fell upon the gathered group as the word went out, "The sluice is open! The drive has started!" Young Frenchmen leaped lightly from one floating log to another, somehow keeping these logs moving away from the bank into the rapid current that was catching the logs and sending them tumbling through the sluice into the foaming icy water below the dam. Many logs, feeling the force of the current, moved on but above the dam others began to crowd and pile up in that dis-order which would cause a jam. Advantage must be taken of the high swift water to "run" the timber.

One young man, who had arrived that very morning to take part in the first day's work, ran nimbly out from the bank, leaping from log to log, pushing and shoving the way-ward timber. Then, without a moment's warning, in fact, before many could see what was happening, he slipped and disappeared into the cold blue river and in the twinkling of an eye the floating logs had covered the spot where he went down.

Loud cries filled the air and the river boss quickly ordered the sluice closed. The hush which fell over the crowd was something to be felt. Suddenly the joy of the day was gone. The very pine trees seemed dark and somber, the spring sunshine seemed cold and a chilling wind struck the faces of the watchers. One had given his life that the purchased possession might reach its destination.

Six weeks later the story was told as the logs bearing the lumbermen's seals were being removed from behind the boom where they awaited their redemption by their owners.[14]

Before they left for Mt. Kineo House, Ethel asked her mother to watch for mail from the American Missionary Association and to forward it to her as soon as it came. One day in mid-July on her afternoon break, the office clerk informed her that a thick envelope had arrived. Ethel rushed to tell Lena, who was finishing up in the dining room. She was certain it was the awaited letter.

"Lena, I have a letter from the American Missionary Association. Come to my room as soon as you're off duty tonight and I'll tell you what it says."

She could hardly wait to open it. Hurrying to her room, she took from the envelope a letter from the AMA Executive Secretary, Dr. James W. Cooper. Enclosed were two application forms, as well as a copy of the *American Missionary*, a newsletter which listed the qualifications for a teaching position.[15]

The letter stated that there were two openings at Chandler Normal School, and the annual salary would be $1,000.[16] The newsletter gave the required qualifications. If interested, they should reply immediately and be prepared to arrive in Lexington by September 15. Room and board would be provided in the teachers' home on the Chandler campus. Self-addressed envelopes were enclosed.

Quickly turning to the newsletter, Ethel read the listed qualifications:

Education: Must be a graduate of Normal School or College.

Character: Must furnish credentials of Christian standing and be of impeccable character. Evangelical Christians preferred, but teachers may be appointed from any Protestant denomination. Must have commitment to aid Freedmen, feel the importance of the work and have their hearts in the cause they represent.

Desirable qualities: Good health, energy, ability to endure hardship, common sense, good personal habits and the ability to get along with colleagues. No one who uses intoxicating drinks or tobacco is employed.

Ethel read it again. "Impeccable character...commitment to aid freedmen...ability to endure hardship." What hardship? Do I have common sense? I hope I can get along with my colleagues...

That evening as soon as her duties were finished in the dining room, Lena hurried to Ethel's room. The girls could hardly contain themselves as they read over the papers that had come.

"Oh, Et," exclaimed Lena, "Just think, we could be in Lexington by September!"

Still certain that this was what they wanted to do, they carefully filled out the applications at the little round table in Ethel's room, and then wrote their resumes of their teaching experience. They hoped the Executive Secretary at the AMA would look upon them favorably. Sealing the envelopes with a prayer, the next morning they asked the desk clerk to please mail them when he went to the Post Office.

As they left the clerk's office, Ethel turned to her friend, "Do you think they'll accept us? They have awfully high standards. We'll be going as real missionaries, you know. Do you think they'll believe we are of impeccable character?"

"Of course, Et. You know, we've always behaved ourselves. And I'm sure our ministers will give us good recommendations. Especially you."

Chapter Four - Chandler's Challenges

As soon as Mt. Kineo House closed for the summer the girls returned to Bucksport. They discussed how long the trip would be to Lexington, their itinerary, their wardrobes, which books to take. They hoped the letter of acceptance would come soon. They had saved their wages and tips during the summer months, anticipating travel and other expenses to that far-off land of Kentucky.

On August 25th, the long-awaited letter came from the American Missionary Association in New York. It was a short note from Dr. Cooper. It said they had been accepted and appointed to teach at Chandler Normal School, Lexington, Kentucky for the 1920-21 school year. Lena was to teach the primary grades, and Ethel the seventh and eighth grades. The letter instructed them to take the Louisville & Nashville train from Cincinnati on the afternoon of September 26, and Mr. F. J. Werking, Director of the school, would meet them at the station.[17]

As Ethel finished reading the letter aloud, she and Lena looked at each other.

"We're going! We're going! And we've got less than a month to get ready! Mama, Mama," she shouted as she headed for the kitchen, "We're going to Kentucky!"

Lena said goodbye the next day and headed for her home in Enfield. She had hoped to sell her Model T Ford to get money for the trip, and was elated when Ethel's brother Vinal, crazy about cars, offered to buy it.

Besides taking lighter clothes for the warmer South, Ethel thought of her beloved books, still in the bottom of the trunk she had brought from Easton. These she had acquired when she was a Normal School student at East Maine Conference Seminary. The classic academic courses had included Latin, Geometry, French, History, and English. Among the books she would take were the five volume *New Students Reference Work* by C. B. Beach; the *How and Why Library* by Eleanor Atkinson; *Government, Its Origin and Growth in the U.S.* by Robert Lansing and Gary M. Jones; *Essentials of Algebra for Secondary Schools* by Webster Wells; *An Introduction to the Study of American Literature* by Brander Matthews, James B. Greenough's *Caesar's Gallic War*. In addition she packed her *Fifth Reader with Introductory Treatise on Elocution* by G. S. Hillard; *A Short History of England's and America's Literature* by E. M. Tappan, and her beloved leather bound *Twenty Beautiful Stories from Shakespeare*. On top she placed that little green velvet covered book, *The Beauty of a Life of Service* by Phillips Brooks. She wasn't sure her students would be ready for these, but she would take them to have on hand and for study. Perhaps the high school or normal department teachers could use them.

She wondered who the other teachers would be. No doubt young people like themselves, thought Ethel, ambitious northerners ready to try their hand at changing the world. Little did she know that one of those teachers was to play a very important part in her life.

44

On September 23 Lena arrived in Bucksport at noon in her Model T, and Vinal was there, grinning broadly, obviously pleased to have

his own car. His dream was to own a gas station and garage in Enfield some day. He handed Lena the $175 he had saved, and Lena handed him the keys.

Vinal was handsome and twenty-one; Ethel suspected he had a girl in mind to court in his newly acquired car. That evening Vinal loaded the girls' trunks into the car, and Lena showed him how to crank the motor.

**Ethel Applebee's brother,
Vinal Applebee.
EVA Collection**

It was soon time to leave. Ethel had said goodbye to her youngest brother, Francis, that morning after breakfast before he left for school. She wasn't surprised when he told her he had made pitcher on the high school baseball team. He had surely practiced enough, constantly throwing that old tattered ball against the barn door!

It was hard to say goodbye to her Mother, who had given her so much support over the years. This mother had moved to Bucksport to work as a matron at the East Maine Conference Seminary earning Ethel's tuition there. Mabel, not given to emotion, could not keep the tears from her eyes or the quiver from her voice as they hugged each other.

"Goodbye, Ethel, write often. I want to know all about that school."

Ethel replied through the tears rolling down her cheeks, "Yes, Mama, I will. And you write too. Tell me all about yourself and the boys."

Vinal had the road mapped out. They arrived in Portland in plenty of time to catch the ferry to Boston. Vinal helped the girls with their trunks and watched on the pier until the steamer, the *Bay State*, eased out of the harbor.[18] It was a beautiful, clear day, the ocean sparkling and very blue. The girls stood at the railing, waving until Vinal was out of sight. It suddenly dawned upon them that this adventure, so long dreamed of, was actually taking place. It was a frightening yet exciting leap from their own comfortable little world into the unknown. Both girls were silent as Portland disappeared in the distance.

This was their first venture into the South. What would be different there? They had never taught Negro children before nor had any contact with members of that race. They had heard stories that White teachers in the South were not readily accepted by either the White adults or the Negro parents. Ethel was glad Lena was with her; she could not have done this alone. Standing there at the railing, looking at the waves, she realized that she was answering a call within her, that deep desire to do her part for the cause of a needy people. She knew the best contribution she could offer was her skill as a teacher.

And she thought of Wellington, who had died years before, and her promise to him.

The *Bay State* glided smoothly into the Boston dock and unloaded. Lena hailed a taxi, which took the girls and their trunks to the train station. It was now nearly two o'clock, and they realized they had not eaten since breakfast. Finding their seats on the Pullman, they opened the lunch Ethel's mother had packed for them. The sandwiches, cookies, gingerbread, and apples tasted good, and the hot tea in the thermos lifted their spirits.

This was their first trip on a Pullman. The porter told them their beds would be made up at 9:30 p.m., even though the train would not pull out until 11:00. Both girls were happy to get into their berths early. Ethel insisted Lena's longer legs would fit better in the lower berth, and so before Lena could object, Ethel climbed into the cramped upper berth. There was little sleep that night for either of them as the train rumbled, clanked and jerked, stopping at every town along the way. It was morning when the train pulled into Buffalo. Discovering that it was possible to see Niagara Falls on their layover in Buffalo, they had arranged for an excursion.

They took the Louisville and Nashville train in Buffalo, which continued through Cleveland to Cincinnati. In Cleveland they re-membered to change their watches back one hour. Their berths were made up early that evening, and they were glad to turn in. Both of them were excited and it was hard to get to sleep, for they realized that tomorrow they would arrive in Lexington!

At 5:30 p.m. September 27, the train pulled into Lexington, a bustling town with many church steeples. Ethel and Lena noticed several Negroes on the streets, which surprised them. These Northern girls had seldom seen Negroes on the streets of the towns and cities of Maine, although they were aware that Maine was foremost in granting Negroes equal civil and political rights.[19]

Weary from their long trip, with clothes rumpled, and long hair loosened from hair pins, the two girls stepped down from the train and immediately felt the warm air of that southern city. There was a difference, too, in the atmosphere, something they could not put their fingers on just then. Coming toward them was a middle-aged couple.

The man was small, with thinning brown hair, wearing horn-rimmed glasses, and dressed in a suit and high collar that made him look very much like a professor. His wife was almost as tall, a little heavier set, with a pleasant, round motherly face.

"Miss Spencer, Miss Applebee? Mr. and Mrs. Werking from Chandler." He extended his hand. "Welcome. We are so glad to see you."

Mr. And Mrs. F. J. Werking, Directors of Chandler Normal School, Lexington, KY.
EVA Collection

"How do you do," replied Ethel, shaking his hand. "We are glad to be here at last. It has been a long trip." They followed the Werkings to a touring car parked across the street, eager to see their new home and Chandler School. They realized they were hungry, too.

As if reading their minds, Mrs. Werking turned to them. "I suppose you have not eaten. Supper will be served as soon as we take you to your rooms. Supper is served daily at 6:15." Mr. Werking shortly turned the car into a driveway leading to a large partly brick and frame house that looked very homelike.

The teacher's home on campus of Chandler Normal School, 1919-1922, Lexington, KY.
EVA Collection

As the wide oak doors swung open, Ethel noticed the crisp white curtains at the windows of the vestibule and the beautiful crystal chandelier hanging from the ceiling. The oak paneling was luxurious, as was the wool green carpet underfoot.[20] They could smell the steak and baked potatoes cooking in the kitchen just off the dining room. What a relief to be here at last.

Mrs. Werking took the girls up a winding front staircase and showed them two large rooms at the top of the stairs. "Miss Applebee, you are to have this corner room, and Miss Spencer, you may take the room next to that. The water closet is down the hall. Freshen up and then come down to the parlor. I want to introduce you to the other teacher."

In Ethel's room were a rocker, a single white iron bed, a bookcase, an oak desk with a chair, a lamp, a dresser, a closet, and a braided oval rug on the floor next to the bed. The dresser had a large, framed mirror. Ethel noticed there was even a small gas stove. The bed was already made up with a white coverlet. Ethel knew she would sleep well that night.

As Mrs. Werking disappeared down the steps leaving the young women to settle into their rooms, Ethel stood in the middle of the floor and marveled at what she saw. She was surprised at the large comfortable rooms. She had never seen anything quite like this in Maine!

Ethel and Lena looked at each other. "Well, Et, here we are. What do you think?"

Ethel smiled wearily, "So far I like it. What a beautiful room! I never dreamed we would have anything as nice as this. Mrs. Werking said we were to meet the other teacher. I wonder where she's from. Are there only three of us?"

As they went down the stairs they saw a short young woman standing with Mrs. Werking. She wore horn-rimmed glasses, her blond hair pulled back in a knot at the nape of her neck. She turned

and smiled as Ethel and Lena descended the steps.

"Miss Applebee, Miss Spencer, let me introduce you to Miss Sara Leighton, also from Maine."

"How do you do," replied Lena. "Just call us Ethel and Lena. So nice to meet another teacher from Maine. What part of Maine are you from?"

"Portland," Sara replied. "Well, actually, Cumberland Center, just outside Portland."

Sara Leighton, teacher at Chandler Normal School, 1919-1922, Lexington, KY.
EVA Collection

The large dining room table was covered with a white linen table cloth and matching napkins, and set with exquisite silver and fine bone china. Clearly Lena and Ethel had better mind their manners and remember which fork and spoon to use! Professor Werking came in then and showed them to their seats. Presently a Colored waiter appeared, immaculately dressed in black trousers, spotless white shirt, and black tie. He served them steak, baked potatoes, spaghetti, and a tomato salad. There were home-cooked rolls, butter, and for dessert, applesauce with cream.

"After supper we'll take you over to the school. I'm sure you girls are eager to see your classrooms and meet some of the staff," Mr. Werking said. "By the way, we'll be bringing your trunks up from the station early tomorrow morning."

The table conversation was pleasant but reserved. Ethel wanted so much to get to know Sara better, and hoped there would be time this evening to visit with her. She seemed so cheerful, easy to know. During the dinner conversation they learned that she had graduated from Farmington Normal School in June, and was several years younger than Ethel and Lena. This would be her first year of teaching (and the hardest, thought Ethel). Sara was assigned to the high school and normal school classes, and would teach home economics. When Ethel learned of Sara's qualifications and noticed her impeccable manners, she was impressed.

The sun was just setting when the three teachers and the Werkings left the dining room and walked together across the green lawns. The campus was furnished with walkways winding among lovely trees and shrubs. Though Ethel spotted none of her beloved pine trees, there were a few hemlock and boxwood. Whoever had planned this school had an eye for beauty and serenity. It was an inviting place to teach. Ethel wondered if the children realized how fortunate they were. What a contrast to the little one-room schools where she had taught in Maine!

Their destination was a large three-story brick building at the center of the campus. On a slight rise, it commanded a beautiful view of the surrounding countryside. Mr. Werking led them into the front hallway, oak paneled and spacious. On the back wall, facing the door, was the portrait of an attractive lady of about fifty, with wavy brown hair and hazel eyes. Mrs. Werking spoke:

"That is Mrs. Phoebe Chandler, our benefactor.[21] She offered the American Missionary Association a sum of money to establish a school for Negro children in Kentucky. As is its practice, the AMA promised to name the school in her honor. It was her generosity that built this school, and so it bears her name. Her funds paid for the four acres you see here as well as the home, and this building. Her additional donations have kept the school running for several years, and we have been blessed indeed by the kindness of this wonderful lady."

Chandler in springtime: Chandler Normal School, Lexington, KY. Courtesy Amistad Research Center, Tulane University, New Orleans, LA.

Lena asked, "Has she been here? Have you met her?"

"No," replied Mrs. Werking, "But we do send her progress reports, and she is very interested in what goes on here."

As they moved to other parts of the building, Mr. Werking said the total enrollment at that time was two hundred, and the tuition was $10 per year for each pupil. He showed them the cloakrooms, wash rooms, a reception hall, recitation rooms, a music room, and a small combination reading room and library. On entering the library, Mr. Werking proudly remarked that it was the largest library possessed by any Colored school in Kentucky.

There were eleven grades in all. The primary grade classrooms where Lena would teach and the seventh and eighth grade rooms where Ethel would teach were on the first floor. The high school and normal school classes were on the second floor. Ethel's classroom was fairly large, with thirty-five desks and several large blackboards. There were windows overlooking baseball and football fields.

Mr. Werking then took them to the third floor and showed them the auditorium and chapel, seating 500.[22] Its magnitude astonished Ethel. She had never thought in terms of so many parents and children gathered in one place. She had the sinking feeling that she was a naive girl from the backwoods of Maine who had a lot to learn. Still, she was grateful for the training in etiquette and social skills learned from her summers at Mt. Kineo, Kamp Conway, and Peaks Isle.

At the close of the tour, Mr. Werking took the new teachers into his office on the second floor. He asked them to be seated in the leather chairs arranged opposite his large mahogany desk. Standing behind the desk, he began by saying:

"As you know by now, Chandler School holds to the highest standards. Not only does the American Missionary Association expect this, but we are agreed that education best takes place where there is discipline along with good instruction from dedicated teachers. The aim of this school is to turn out scholars who can, in turn, teach their own people."

Mr. Werking paused, sat down with hands folded on top of the desk, and continued:

"We expect our pupils to be proficient, not only in the usual courses of study, but also in music and public speaking. We encourage their participation in performances given to the community, plays, concerts, speaking contests throughout the school year.[23] You, as their teachers, will determine how well they, and Chandler, succeed in these goals. For that reason we are happy with the qualifications you three teachers bring to Chandler.[24] I believe you will fit in well here, and I heartily welcome each of you."

With a warm smile he stood and shook hands with each one. "I know you are weary from your long journey. Since I have work to do here, Mrs. Werking will take you back to your home. Let's meet here again tomorrow at three after you have had a chance to work in your classrooms. We'll discuss in more detail the regulations and expectations we have for teachers here. Good evening. I will see you tomorrow."

Although tired and a little overwhelmed at all they had seen and heard the last few hours, Ethel took time to write a short note to her mother that evening when she returned to her room:

September 27, 1920

Dear Mama,

I suppose you have received all the cards I sent along the way. Sent the last one from the station in Lexington before we came up to the school. Mr. and Mrs. Werking are nice and pleasant. They came down to meet us. My trunk hasn't been brought up yet; it will be in the morning. The fourth teacher for some reason did not join us, so thus far there are only three of us, Sara Leighton, Lena and me. Sara is only 21 and this is her first teaching job. I think I am going to like her. This whole place looks very much like the snapshots I had. We have dinner at night at our "home." I have a nice corner room, two big windows, two electric lights, a funny little gas stove, good closet, white iron bed, bare floor with rug in front of bed and another at foot, a rocker, straight chair, mirror, dresser, a fine writing desk, larger than yours, and a little book case.

We have dinner at night. Had steak, baked potatoes, spaghetti with cheese and tomato salad, bread and butter, applesauce with cream.

Have met a good many of the Colored people, the boys all seem to look alike and the girls the same but think I will be able to tell them by their clothes.

Wish you would send my napkin ring. I forgot it. I had $6 left of $78 when I got here this morning.

Mrs. Werking has just been opening a mission barrel and a lot of the Negroes have been in buying.

Hope you have got the house shingled and that everybody has got over their various forms of disease.

Love, Ethel

Later in the week Ethel took time to write again, describing their excursion to Niagara Falls:

Dear Mama:

Our excursion to see Niagara Falls was beautiful. The sun came out and there was a rainbow on both the American and Canadian sides. The Canadian side, I think, is better than ours. Later in the day we ate a nice supper in a little restaurant near the falls: roast chicken, celery, sweet pota-toes, little biscuits and oranges for dessert. On the way back to the train station we passed the famous "Home of Shredded Wheat" and it looked just like it does on the cereal boxes. We did not take time to go in. But we did take time to visit St. Joseph's Cathedral, the most beautiful of churches, lovely colored windows, and it is immense.

Makes you feel like whispering it is so dim, with the light coming through the stained glass windows.

Love, Ethel

Breakfast was to be served at 7:00 a.m., and so Ethel set her windup alarm clock for 6:00 and was up when a knock came at her door. It was Sara, bright and cheery, pretty in the long, blue middie dress that matched her eyes. "Ready for breakfast, Ethel? Lena says she will be right along."

"I'm as ready as I'll ever be, I guess. Do I look all right? All my things are in my trunk at the station. I hope they bring it up soon. When did you come?"

"I arrived two days ago, so I haven't been here much longer than you. We'll soon get acquainted," Sara replied reassuringly. "Everyone is as nice as they can be. And you look just fine."

Lena joined them on the stairs, and the girls went down to breakfast. Mrs. Werking came out of the kitchen with the cook, a middle-aged Colored woman.

"This is Hattie, our cook. This is Miss Applebee, Miss Spencer and Miss Leighton."

"Pleased to meet you," she said cordially, and disappeared into the kitchen.

The girls waited a moment until Mr. Werking arrived. He took his place at the head of the table, with Mrs. Werking at the other end. Two of the three girls sat on one side of the table and one on the opposite side, which left one chair vacant.

As they were eating, Mr. Werking explained the morning routine. "Each of you girls will take a turn at coming down early in the morning to set the table for breakfast, and you will again be expected to help with the evening meal at 6:15. Lunch is served at noon. Since the children go home for lunch; you have an hour to eat your lunch here and to be back in your classrooms by one o'clock. You will see a schedule of your breakfast duty posted in the kitchen. You will not be expected to help with other meals or on weekends."

Lena ventured a question about the vacant chair at the table. "Is there another teacher coming?"

Mr. Werking replied, "We had hoped to have a teacher come this week from Richmond. But she has sickness in her family... her mother, I believe. We hope she will be able to come before school opens. Her name is Katherine Lewis.[25] She taught here last year."

After breakfast the three teachers excused themselves, eager to get to work in their classrooms. Ethel found a good supply of textbooks but had to ask about supplies for the children—pencils, composition books, paper, and, for the upper grades, ink bottles and pens. They could get these from a small storage closet on the second floor. Sam, the Negro janitor, had the key.

Hearing the sound of children's voices, Ethel looked out of her window. There were several children playing on the playground below, shooting baskets into a bare hoop. She saw other children of various sizes coming up the front walk with their mothers. Ethel took note that not one White child was among them, and then remembered this was a school exclusively for Negro children.[26] They are why we are here, thought, Ethel. I love the sound of their voices. Mr. Werking greeted and registered the children as they came, and then brought them to their classrooms where they met their teachers.

Mrs. Werking mentioned that she would be working in a large room at the back of the building that morning, sorting and distributing donated clothing. She invited the three teachers to come and take a look at her "store" whenever they had time. Today the store would be open from nine until noon. After registering their children, several parents went around to the back of the building to buy clothing from Mrs. Werking.

That evening Ethel wrote to her mother:

I met a good many of the Colored people today. I am glad I got to meet some of them before school opens. All of them seemed to be a little shy of me, but that may change when I get thirty or forty of them in the room together. Mrs. Werking opened mission barrels today and a lot of the Negroes have been buying. School opens next week. Have worked all day getting ready. Glad I brought my books along. They seem to have a good supply of books here, though, which somewhat surprised me. Guess Mrs. Chandler thought of that, too.

I will try to write each week.

Love, Ethel

Ethel, as well as Lena, was eager to know what the "regulations and expectations" were that Mr. Werking would explain that afternoon. She worked in her room all that day, arranging desks, making lesson plans, noting additions to the class lists that had come to her from Mr. Werking. It would take a while to match names with faces.

The teachers gathered in the office promptly at three that afternoon. Seated behind his large desk, Mr. Werking again welcomed them and asked if everything was in order in their classrooms, and if they needed anything. Lena said one of her windows would not open and asked if the janitor could help. Sara asked if the gas stove on her floor was operating; she had not been able to get it to light. Mr. Werking said he would have Samuel look at it. Ethel was satisfied with her room and its furnishings, but asked how many students she would have, as the roll was now at thirty-five and that was the number of desks she had.

Mr. Werking told Ethel he would see that she got more desks if needed. He continued to address the teachers:

"Young ladies, you are part of an education crusade which Mr. W. E. B. Du Bois called the Tenth Crusade. He said it 'was the finest thing in American history, and one of the few things not tainted with sordid greed and cheap vainglory.'"[27] Mr. Werking continued:

"The American Missionary Association believes that whatever the text, your duty is to apprize Negro youth of their responsibilities to God, country, family and society. These things are just as important as teaching academics. You will open the class each morning with patriotic songs, and throughout the day teach good manners, truthfulness, punctuality and hard work. You are expected to teach morality with your subjects. I am sure you have done this before, but I just want to remind you of the importance with which these standards are held by the AMA."[28]

Mr. Werking continued: "You will find there is need for strict discipline here, as many of the children have little at home. You are expected to be as strict as you need to be and require pupils to obey you. When they do not obey, it is allowed that you administer corporal punishment when necessary. For severe incidents, please send the student to me. I will see that the student is dealt with appropriately. In the past, the method of discipline which works best, and I have used it often, is the threat of expulsion. The parents hold it as a great honor to have their children in Chandler. As you know, until a Negro high school is built in Lexington, we are the only school with upper grades open to these children. To be expelled is a blow to their dignity. Please keep me informed of any real problems you have. Remember, too, that this is a different culture from what you knew in the North. Your patience will be tried and tested, but you must keep the upper hand and, while being strict, be kind. These children will surprise you with their accomplishments and abilities before the school year is out.

"We are to have a Physical Training teacher here once a week. Other days you will teach it. The music teacher is also to come once a week and will teach in the music room. You will be given a schedule as to when you are to send children to her. So far, we have not heard from Katherine Lewis. I hope she will come soon.

"Oh yes, the school day begins at nine and ends at three-thirty. A bell will ring when classes are to move from one area to another. You have one hour for lunch. You should be in your rooms by 8:30 each morning. Do you have any questions now?"

Lena spoke up, "What do you mean by corporal punishment? Are we to administer that?"

Mr. Werking paused before answering: "In the past, when teachers could not coax students into good behavior, directors of AMA schools occasionally resort to using a rod or switch. That would be my decision to make. I do not believe parents object to this, because they very much want their children to behave well, to learn and succeed in school."[29]

Ethel spoke up, "Do the parents of the Negro children object to northern White teachers teaching their children? Will they accept us?"

"Miss Applebee, there are drawbacks to seeking a teaching career in the South. You will not be accepted socially by many Whites here. That is to be expected. However, I believe by being a good teacher, dedicated to the students, you will find cautious acceptance among most of the parents. While we do not force ourselves upon them socially, there may be times when they will invite you to their homes, and they will consider it an honor if you accept such an invitation. The three of you may find that the only social life you have here is with each other, and of course with other teachers who may come."[30]

On Monday, October 3, 1920, the evening before school opened, Ethel wrote:

Dear Mama,

Yesterday afternoon, which was Saturday, we went for a ride with the Werkings in their touring car out in the country. We passed two big stock farms, one of which raised the famous race horses, Peter the Great and Dan Patch. You wouldn't think any of these places were farms in passing. A good many are all fenced off in which we would maybe call a lane, really long narrow pastures, etc. where are kept the colts with their mothers, each in their own pasture.

Everywhere we have been it seems like a big grove, no underbrush nor small trees. We saw horses and cows feeding under the trees and back in the distance you could see a house. The cattle appear to do the lawn mowing. Haven't seen any real woods though.

I have been glad to wear my big coat when out driving. Last Saturday we headed for the Kentucky River, got out there seven miles, broke a front spring of the Ford and we all had to walk back to the city where we got a streetcar for home. We are a mile and a quarter from downtown. The city hasn't as large a population as Portland, but it is quite lovely. Blossoms and tulips are all in bloom.

We've all worked hard getting ready for the opening of school. Everyone is very helpful, and it's great to have Lena here to laugh and cry with, and Sara, too, seems awfully nice. She fits right in and is very efficient. You should see her room. She teaches home economics and she has arranged her rooms to look like a kitchen and dining room. We're going to be very crowded in my room, and that may cause problems. I'll probably have to square my jaw and use my sternest voice. Think of me this week.

Love, Ethel

Chapter Five - Classes and Extracurricular Activities

Ethel, as well as the other teachers, soon discovered what Mr. Werking meant by "tested and tried." Just as she had feared, the first week of school tested her endurance to the limit. She wrote about it on the following Sunday afternoon:

Dear Mama,

Your letters received and the ones you forwarded all right. Haven't had a minute when I could write you before, as this has been a very busy week.

We began school in earnest on Monday, October 5th. Different students have been coming in and now I have my room full with three more expected this week. That will make about 36 or 38. Four sit in chairs and one sits at a desk in the back of the room, so don't know just what I shall do with the others when they come as my room is full all the way down to my desk, and there is a big coal heater in the back. You see, the room isn't big enough. They are most all girls, only two boys in the seventh grade and five in the eighth so far, so with the room packed full of acting girls I have had a time of it. A good many of them are lazy and all noisy and laugh all the time at everything I say, even when I roar at them in my school marm voice.[31]

Mr. Werking has strange punishment. Two of mine who bothered me too much yesterday I took to him and told him I wanted them punished every noon for a week, and he sent them out pulling weeds! They refuse to do a thing without being told at least six times. Never mind anybody. Lena said that a new teacher never expected to be able to stay in a room more than a couple of hours. However, I swore I would stay and have so far, even though the noise was terrific. Guess I'll get them in time. Way below grade in every subject. Seventh grade don't {sic} know all of the tables, none of them can do much in long division, nor are they at all sure about fractions.

Tell Mrs. Buck that Hannah Buck of the Island always sends things to this school. Her aunt, isn't it? Good many people send barrels of clothing, second hand shoes, hats, anything. If you folks want to clean up the attics, get together and send a barrel here. I must be up early in the morning and ready to go at it again, so will say goodnight. Ethel

Another letter mentions discipline problems that Ethel encountered that fall. She was finally able to "conquer" the class and gain reasonable control so that she could do the teaching she so much loved to do.

October 25, 1920

Dear Mama:

It was very cold here for about a week; we have even had a little white frost. Have had to start fires in the school rooms two different mornings, but today is lovely and warm. I had a cold the first of my being here, but am all over it now. It is pleasant all around the house. Trees, grass and flowers and everything as green as June. On our few trips outside of the city once in a while we see a few trees turned by the frost.

Katherine Lewis, the other teacher, came the second week of school; guess her mother is much better. Then a Colored teacher came, the second week, Laura Carroll.[32] She is about the largest woman I have ever seen, but is jolly and lots of fun. She teaches the smallest children and they all love her.

I am going to try to get a snapshot of my room, and of the children anyway, to send you soon.

I used the old flat rule on the hind ends of one little boy and one of the smallest girls. Got one of the Colored teachers to come in so there would be no trouble.

I took one of the girls by the back of the neck a while ago, and she tried to hit me. I closed up a little tighter on the cords of her neck and my finger nail, being sharp, scratched her. Then she quit and so did I, but she brought her mother back with her at noon. After talking it over she sent her daughter to Mr. Werking herself for a strapping. They get the idea that you punish them just because they are Colored. It is quite the opposite. Because they are Colored we can't touch them. Goodbye for now. Ethel

P.S. The first football game comes off here on campus this Friday. Four of my larger boys are on the team. You don't need to put anything on your letters but the street number. Remember me to all the neighbors.

One Saturday while helping to sort donated clothing with Mrs. Werking, Ethel asked her how it was that they had been provided such lovely rooms on campus, and the Negro teachers lived elsewhere. Mrs. Werking explained, "One of the reasons Chandler School provides a home on campus for northern teachers is because there are no White homes that will board "nigger" teachers, as they are sometimes called. While it is possible for Negro teachers to find rooms to rent in Negro homes, this is not socially acceptable for White teachers. The American Missionary Association is very strict about the decorum of their teachers. After the Civil War, ostracism by the Southern Whites was rampant, even to violence, against White persons who were friendly to Negroes. Things have improved since then, but it still prevails in many parts of the South."[33]

The white teachers at Chandler with Directors Mr. and Mrs. F. J. Werking: Ethel Applebee, Sara Leighton, Lena Spencer: Katherine Lewis, 1920-21.
EVA Collection

The black teachers at Chandler Normal School, 1920-21.
EVA Collection

Ethel, Lena, Sara, and Katherine felt the rejection keenly. They were scarcely spoken to or acknowledged on the streets of Lexington and only minimally by clerks when they had to purchase something in stores, or went into the Post Office.

Laura Carroll and Maggie Smith, the Negro teachers at Chandler, accepted the three Northern teachers without prejudice. Their friend-liness made it possible for the White teachers to have connections with the Negro community.[34] Laura Carroll invited Ethel to go with her to visit some of the children in their homes, an offer she was happy to accept. Ethel wrote in one of her weekly letters home: *"Have been in a number of homes."*

In another letter she wrote that fall: *"We are all invited down to the home of one of the Colored teachers this afternoon."*

Weekends gave Ethel welcome respite from the demanding weekly schedule of preparing lessons, teaching, and attempting to control the pupils' behavior. Though sewing was not one of her strong points, on a free Saturday she went downtown and bought material to make a new shirtwaist and skirt for herself. On Friday evenings she and the other teachers went to the football games if held on campus, or sometimes they got a ride to a game in another town. Her early letters to her mother described some of her extracurricular activities.

November 1, 1920

Dear Mama:

I have had no letter from you for a while, so will try to write a bit more.

This morning was all spent in getting a skirt basted up, ready to stitch. It is brown and black cotton stuff, rather pretty. Just had a snapshot in my best dress, which will send you if it turns out good. It is navy tricolette, same thing as a diagonal serge, accordion pleated skirt, red patent leather belt and collar and cuffs of gold, blue, red and little beads. Hope you get the idea.

71

The football game was at Winchester on Friday this week, forty miles away, so none of us could go. But we did get a car and went for a ride. You will know how crowded we were when I tell you that Lena and I are the lightest of the lot and one teacher weighs 215 pounds. We had lots of fun and felt better for the outing. It gets sort of tiresome if one just sticks right to school work all the time.

We have been to the Opera House twice. Once to a musical comedy, <u>Dear Me</u>, which was very good. Last Saturday we saw <u>Rainbow Girl</u>, but didn't care for it.

Can't write more as I must call the music teacher and do some school work and it is six o'clock now. Love to the boys and everyone.

Ethel

548 Georgetown Street, Lexington

November 8, 1920

Dear Mama:

Your letter received latter part of the week. I sent the post cards in place of letter as have been so busy.

Have had to stay with late students the past week. Each teacher has a week at it. Stay with them in a downstairs room during chapel and a half hour after school while they make up time. Haven't had time to even go downtown for almost two weeks.

Week ago Saturday we all went to Paris with the students and football boys for a game. About forty of us went by special trolley. It is about twenty miles down there. Had the best time and our boys won 6 to 0. Last Saturday we played here with Louisville High for championship of the state, but lost, 4l to 0. I helped sell candy till almost dark. I sold tickets the first game here three weeks ago. Also helped make it. I mean the candy.

Had an awful week last week. I kept some of them after school 'til 4:45 one night. They assured me that they would "pay me up" for that. But they are very changeable and next day were good as pie. Four of my boys play football. I only have nine.

The great big one is full of the old Harry. Can't help liking him. Is fifteen but straight and well formed. Wears soldiers' trousers with his legs all bound up to make leggings. Weighs one-sixty. One day during a study period when everything was nice and still he suddenly looked up and said, "Miss Applebee, don't you want a chair so you can sit down?" I had to thank him, but of course I refused.

Love,

Ethel

A student on campus of Chandler Normal School, 1920-21.
EVA Collection

Chapter Six - Elocution Contests and Christmas

Ethel enjoyed public speaking. She had participated in several LTL (Little Temperance League) and WCTU (Woman's Christian Temperance Union) speaking contests in elementary and high school, winning several medals.[35] Wherever she had taught in Maine, as well as at Chandler, she encouraged her pupils to memorize and recite narrative poems for special programs. One of her instructions to speech pupils was, "Always know the meaning of a selection or poem before memorizing it."

As Mr. Werking walked past Ethel's classroom one day he heard her reciting to the children, "The Midnight Ride of Paul Revere." A few days later he called Ethel into his office and asked if she would be interested in sponsoring the Demorest Medal Speaking Contests at Chandler. He went on to explain what that meant.

"The American Missionary Association has always required the teaching of temperance in their schools. These contests not only promote pure temperance sentiments and habits among the pupils, but often secure pledges of total abstinence from the use of all intoxicating liquors and tobacco by the participants as well as the audience. You will remember this was one of the requirements for your employment by the AMA."[36]

He further explained, "We plan to have five contests during the school year. The first one is to be held on Saturday, December 12, in the school chapel. There will be four such contests at which the winner will receive a silver medal. At the last contest, which will be held at the graduation exercises, the four silver medalists will compete for the cherished gold medal. Usually the oratorical exercises are interspersed with musical numbers, also rendered by our children. Of course, the music teacher will be in charge of these."

He continued, "You will choose the best speakers of the school, helping them select their essays from material provided by the Demorest Bureau in New York.[37] You may work this into your regular public speaking classes, if you like. I am sure the other teachers will be able to recommend children to you. Will you do it?"

Ethel's blue eyes lighted with excitement. It pleased her that Mr. Werking had taken note of her talents. "Why, yes, Professor, I would like to. But we'd need to get started right away. There isn't much time."

Mr. Werking smiled at Ethel's enthusiasm. "I have the material here. It came in the mail yesterday from Demorest headquarters." He handed Ethel a large brown envelope.

"Thank you, Ethel, for taking on this added responsibility. I have every confidence you and the children will make the school proud."

She took the material to her room. She read it through, and as she did so she pictured which of her children she would choose for the contest. Jane, Lucy and Tom, and of course Robert, her best student, would all do well.

Later, Sara came in and Ethel told her about the contest. She was excited too. "This is grand, Ethel. Just what some of mine need to build their confidence." She gave Ethel four names of possible candidates from the high school and normal school classes.

Hearing the enthusiastic voices in Ethel's room, Lena poked her head in the door to see what was going on.

"Ethel's in charge of speech contests. Professor asked her today," replied Sara.

"Et, you're just the one for the job! Sara, perhaps you didn't know, but Ethel here is quite a speaker herself. I've heard her do several pieces that made my hair stand on end. Do one for us now, Et." She took a seat beside Sara on the bed. Just then Katherine and the new teacher, Ella, looked in.

"What's all the excitement about?" asked Katherine..

"We are just about to hear Ethel recite, girls. Come on in and take a chair." The two teachers came in and took seats, one on the rocker and one on the straight chair.

"Now, what will it be, Et?"

Taking her place in the center of the room, Ethel announced very seriously, "Invictus," by William E. Henley. Standing tall, arms relaxed at her side, her chin up, Ethel intoned in her most dramatic style:

> Out of the night that covers me
>> Black as the pit from pole to pole,
> I thank whatever gods may be
>> For my unconquerable soul.
> In the fell clutch of circumstance
>> I have not winced nor cried aloud.

Under the bludgeonings of chance

My head is bloody, but unbowed.

Beyond this place of wrath and tears

Looms but the horror of the shade,

And yet the menace of the years

Finds, and shall find, me unafraid.

It matters not how strait the gate,

How charged with punishments the scroll,

I am the master of my fate,

I am the captain of my soul.

The teachers applauded loudly. Ethel bowed and smiled. "Another, another," cried Sara.

Ethel thought a moment and then said, "I'll do a longer one, if I can remember it. How about "Paul Revere's Ride?""

In her strong, melodious voice Ethel began again:

Listen my children, and you shall hear

Of the midnight ride of Paul Revere,

On the eighteenth of April, in seventy-five

Hardly a man is now alive,

Who remembers that famous day and year...

On and on she went, through all thirteen verses, never missing a word. The teachers listened in rapt attention.

Ethel continued:

So through the night rode Paul Revere

And so through the night went his cry of alarm

To every Middlesex village and farm

A cry of defiance, and not of fear

A voice in the darkness, a knock at the door,

And a word that shall echo forevermore;

For borne on the nightwind of the past,

Through all our history to the last,

In the hour of darkness and peril and need,

The people will waken and listen to hear

The hurrying hoofbeats of that steed,

And the midnight message of Paul Revere.[38]

"Bravo, Bravo!" the teachers cried in unison. "Wonderful!"

"Oh, I think I hear Mrs. Werking calling one of us to come help downstairs. That will have to be all for now, girls," Ethel said as she moved toward the door. "Thank you for listening. We'd all better get ready for supper."

"Promise you'll recite more, Ethel, when you have time." said Sara. "What a talent!"

"Yes," said Katherine. "I want to hear more. How about the 'Wreck of the Hesperus?' Do you know that one?"

"Yes," replied Ethel as she led the way down the stairs. "I learned that years ago. Perhaps another day."

Ethel was pleased with her assignment as speech contest sponsor. She planned to take each child aside, explain the contest, and help him choose his recitation. This was going to be fun for both the children and for her. She decided to work the contest participants into her speech classes, held each Tuesday and Thursday afternoon.

The next morning, before Lena was up, Ethel went to her door, knocked loudly and called out,

"So here hath been dawning another blue day.

Think! Wilt thou let it slip useless away?"

Lena jumped out of bed and opened the door, bleary eyed, hair askew and falling around her shoulders. There was Ethel, all agrin, and they had a good laugh before Ethel bounded down the steps to help with breakfast.

Before Professor Werking approached her, Ethel was teaching public speaking in connection with her English lessons. She began with such poems as "Your Flag and My Flag," "Abou Ben Adhem," "Gradation,"… She could just hear Robert's deep resonant voice as he said: "Heaven is not reached by a single bound,/ but we build the ladder by which we rise,/ from the lowly earth to the vaulted skies,/ and we mount to the summit round by round…"

She took them on to her longer favorites: "The Village Blacksmith," Longfellow's "A Psalm of Life," "Barbara Fritchie," and "O Captain, My Captain." These built their confidence and poise. Now they were ready to concentrate on their selected contest speeches. She'd have the contest participants recite before their class, and then they would be ready to speak before the entire school. In keeping with her belief that children speak well when they understand what they are talking about, she was careful to explain the meaning contained in their recitations.

As she had anticipated, many of the children showed exceptional talent in public speaking and enjoyed outdoing each other in class recitations. And, she thought, it would give those who "talked much but had nothing to say," as Papa used to quote, an opportunity to put their verbosity to use.

A couple of weeks later she took Tom, Lucy, Jane and Robert aside after school and gave them the contest material. Temperance was not a new subject to the children of Chandler. They had heard it often discussed within the walls of the school, so it seemed a natural thing to give speeches on that subject. As they practiced with her privately she coached them on pronunciation, articulation, and expression. They worked hard, wanting to do well in the contest, and to please their teacher.

Lucy's talk was "Why I Will Never Drink," Tom chose "The Bad Effects of Alcohol," and Robert selected "Sobriety, the Way to Success." Jane memorized a dramatic poem, "A Voice from the Poorhouse." In addition to their ability in speaking, Ethel was amazed at the earnestness and sincerity with which they spoke. She had a notion that some were speaking from unpleasant first-hand experience with the effects of alcohol in their homes. Hard work and daily practice by the children prepared them for the December 12 contest. By Thanksgiving vacation they were almost ready. Ethel wrote home on November 18:

Dear Mama,

I started to write you Monday, but have had no time to finish the letter. The reason I have been so busy is I have been training some of my children for a temperance speech contest to be held Dec. 12. They do real well.

Monday night we went to hear the Williams Singers. They are a group of Colored people. They sang at the large Methodist church. Most of the audience were Colored people; only a small section reserved for white people.

I hope the boys have good luck on their hunting trip. Perhaps you'll be having venison for Thanksgiving. We have had frost a few times, but it always comes off as soon as the sun is up. We all wore white dresses to the football game on Saturday. There are still plenty of green leaves and grass. No sign of winter yet. We will have three or four days recess at Thanksgiving time.

I have put two of my seventh graders back to sixth grade, and two up to the High School, so now have thirty-three in my room. Am writing at school while waiting for the gong to ring, so will make it short and will send the other part along from over at my room. Guess this will be all for now. Tell Mrs. Buck I got her letter and was glad to hear from her. Love to all.

Ethel

The morning after Thanksgiving she wrote again:

Dear Mama,

Your letter received first of this week. Suppose you and the boys have received my Thanksgiving cards. If your Sunday School children want to write to the students here, just have them begin with "Dear Friend." Send the whole bunch to me and I will give them out.

Don't know what I have not answered. My skirt came out good. Mrs. Werking had a nice box from Aunt Hannah about a week ago. Mrs. Mann is unduly worried about me. My association with the Colored people will not injure me in the least. We don't think of them as "Niggers," and never use the word here. It is similar to calling a white person "a son of a b—, so of course it doesn't do to use it.

Oh, we all are great friends of this Colored teacher. She is the best company. Can sing, read, play the ukelele or however you spell it, and comical! We all spent Sunday afternoon at her home, talking, playing games and music. Then she served refreshments, lovely white cake and Jell-O with a white sauce of some kind. Don't get whipped cream here. We had a nice turkey dinner yesterday. Today is a holiday. No school again till Monday.

After dinner yesterday we girls all turned to and washed the dishes, dried them and put them away, which was fun as we all did it together. It seemed to please the Werkings. They sat in the parlor, looking a little uneasy with nothing to do for a change. After we were finished in the kitchen Sara reminded me that I had promised to do another one of my recitations some time. So I surprised them with "Lasca." Remember that one? That was the longest and the hardest I ever did. That seemed to top off the day so we got to our rooms fairly early. It is beginning to feel like home here, but I did miss you yesterday, and the boys.

We send out our wash every Wednesday morning. A boy calls for it. It gets back on Friday, all starched and ironed as I have never seen clothes done. One woman does the work for all of us here.

The cook is a young woman who comes in days. Has her own home a little distance up the "pike," as they say. (There are no roads here!) Then there is a girl who helps her, and so earns something toward her school expenses. They have to buy all books and supplies.

No, I never hear from Papa.

Don't see but what there are just as bad white boys or worse, for nobody has ever struck me in the face and am not at all afraid they will. In fact, they are better than white children, for nobody has ever absolutely refused to obey, although sometimes it takes time to convince them. They are always polite, boys always pull their caps right off when they speak to anybody, always say "Good morning, how are you?" If you speak to one on the campus he always takes his hat off while talking to you. One of my boys, the big one, has been elected captain of the basketball team.

I hope the boys had success on their hunting trip. Did they get a deer? Guess I will close now. Want to clean up the trash around my room. Didn't go to breakfast this morning. Am going to write Mrs. Buck before Monday.

Can't find any unanswered questions and have looked over three old letters of yours. Hope all are well and that the boys are home.

Lovingly,

Ethel

The speech contest on December 12 went off exceptionally well. Ethel was nervous for some of the students, since this was their first public speaking, but they surprised her with their confidence. Each spoke clearly and with feeling, something she had instilled in them, and not a word was forgotten. Mrs. Werking, Ella Ross, and Sara were the judges. Robert spoke with natural eloquence and, as Ethel suspected, he came out the winner. He grinned from ear to ear as his name was announced. Proudly he walked to the chapel platform, handsome and tall, as Mr. Werking presented him with the silver medal. Now he would compete in June for the gold! The other competitors still had a chance to go for the gold, for they could enter the other contests to be held in February and in the spring.

Just as Mr. Werking had said at the beginning of the school year, these children showed promise. Some of them surprised Ethel, and as a sensitive teacher she saw abilities that had lain dormant, waiting to be tapped by the touch of a person who dared to challenge them.

Ethel was determined to bring out the best in each one or die trying. Some days were rough; some days she felt no progress was made at all. Other times as she laid her head on her pillow at night her heart sang at how a particular child had done exceptionally well. Those were the days she lived for. It was helpful that she had visited in some of their homes; parents respected her, and when she asked that they help their children with homework, or be sure they got to school on time, they did what she asked. There were other children, of course, who had little support at home, and to these she gave her special attention. Her efforts were paying off; the students were making her proud. She looked forward to the end of the term, when by their accomplishments and good grades they would make Chandler Normal School just as proud.

The same thoughts and feelings were undoubtedly going on in the hearts of Lena, Sara, Katherine, Maggie, and Laura. They also were fine teachers with high standards and would not allow mediocre performance when a child could excel. Many of the children were exceedingly bright. Ethel believed that Robert was a gifted speaker. Perhaps he would become a minister, or a teacher, or both.

Ethel was glad she had decided to come here. Though it was hard work, there were rewards. Perhaps she realized that the experience also was changing her into a mature master teacher, highly thought of by the Director as well as her peers. And she was becoming increasingly fond of the students assigned to her.

December was busy, as teachers prepared the children for the annual Christmas program. Then there would be time off for the holiday. Ethel always enjoyed Christmas, but this year it was hard to be so far from family. She lovingly purchased gifts for each member of her family and mailed a Christmas box early enough for them to receive it before December 25.

Group of children and parents at Chandler Normal School, 1921.
EVA Collection

On December 18 she wrote to her Mother:

548 Georgetown Street

Lexington, Kentucky

Dear Mama:

Your letter received a week or so ago and Clarence's a couple of days ago, so think it time I wrote you a little.

Well, everything is as busy as usual. School closes on Wednesday noon for 10 days vacation. Exams will take up all of the week and then it's time to make out rank cards. Have to do that every month here so as it is always nearer six weeks than four when everyone gets them ready, then it is almost time to begin again.

To answer your question, the inside of the Negro's hands are not white like ours, neither are they black, but look the way ours do after blacking the stove without having gloves on, sort of black and white, black in the lines and under the nails but the rest is fairly white.

Had a letter from Papa and one from Aunt Abbie a few days ago. Have you received the Christmas box? I sent it good and early, about two weeks ago, I believe, so you would surely get it on time. I addressed it to you but there are things for everyone inside. Clarence may be home for Christmas. I take it from his writing that he was not yet able to go back to work.[39] I put Papa's and his in with yours, and the boys' too, as thought you might all be home.

School goes about the same. I sent one girl home for good on Friday. Am not going to have her at all this year. Some days the children are all right, but maybe just as I am settling down with the feeling that at last they are going to do the proper thing they let loose worse than ever. So I have come to the conclusion that they can't be depended upon very much, at least not yet. Great trouble is that they have never been obliged to mind anybody. In the lower grades with the Colored teachers they are worse than in my room.

There is another teacher coming to begin next term. She will help in the high school work. There is just one teacher in that room, (Sara), trying to teach all four years of the course except a few classes that go to Mr. Werking, and two to Lena. Sara teaches Child Study and Pedagogy to the ones who are taking Normal Training. Besides that, the lower grades go into her room for penmanship.

All of us have to teach Physical Training in our own room. Lena teaches it to the high school. Some nights I am more tired than others, but we have a pleasant home, good things to eat and nice rooms, so it might be much worse. In fact, it will be easy for me (that is, easier than it would have been at Ft. Fairfield, at least),[40] if I ever get them tamed or can trust them at all.

Thursday was Lena's birthday and we had a party for her. Mrs. Werking gives everyone a party on their birthday so we have nice times then. We eat by candlelight and have the dining room all fixed up prettily with the favorite colors of the person for whom we are having the party. Then we get a flash light picture of it, like the Hallowe'en one I sent you.

On Wednesday we are going to have a little Christmas program for Chapel as we did for Thanksgiving. Two of my girls are to have a little dialogue and five or six of them are to read original stories which they wrote for English. They are Christmas stories and real good ones, too. Some of the others will have recitations, songs, etc. On Christmas afternoon we have a "tree" at the school for the children. We have our "tree" here on Christmas eve. Then there is one at the Colored people's church some time, don't know just when, that we will attend, as that is our Sunday School. Mrs. Werking has planned a little program there. We all have to give a present to our class. I have only one pupil in my class, so it'd not be very expensive for yours truly. I think I will get her a little Negro doll I saw in a store last week. We don't have such dolls up North.

Wish I could be home for Christmas but can't so will make the best of it. I guess the Werkings and the other teachers are my family here, and I'm lucky to have them. Best Christmas wishes to all.

Ethel

Living room of Teachers' Home decorated for Christmas, 1920.
EVA Collection

Ten days of vacation gave the teachers a much needed rest. The two Colored teachers went home for Christmas.

Ethel wrote a letter on December 26:

Dear Mama,

Hope you have by now received both of my short letters so you won't be worried any longer. My one Sunday School scholar has been sick with whooping cough so for a number of Sundays I haven't had to go. We are going to church later today.

It is just like spring here this morning. Sun shining, windows open, no need to wear rubbers or boots, nor fasten up one's coat when walking.

For Christmas Lena gave me a lovely silk petticoat. Mr. and Mrs. Werking gave us each their photo, my friend, Alice sent me a crocheted yoke, a linen handkerchief and a little calendar. Mrs. Fuller sent a handkerchief and so did Mrs. Buck. The Colored teachers sent the bunch of us two big Christmas cakes and Mr. Packard sent a year's subscription to the "Ladies Home Journal."

After dinner we were invited out for the afternoon, so am just finishing this on Monday morning.

We had an inch or so of snow so it is very nasty out as it has rained enough to make it slushy and slippery. We expect a new teacher by the end of the week. She comes from Min-

neapolis and will help with High School. Another girl who taught here some time ago is coming to visit the last of the week, so we have quite a lot to look forward to. Then we are all invited to the homes of the other teachers some time before school opens.

Will have to be sick so I can wear that pretty new boudoir cap you sent! Must close and get this in the morning's mail. Hope you had a Merry Xmas. Happy New Year and love to all.

Ethel

After the Christmas break even more subjects were added to Ethel's already full schedule. She wrote to her mother: *I am also teaching Bible in school, and Agriculture, in addition to everything else. Forgotten how many subjects that makes, but it is quite a few.*

The American Missionary Association saw no problem with religion being taught in their schools. They believed that religion and education complement each other. They said "The Negroes need educated Christianity and they must have Christianized education to get it... To achieve this most desirable and necessary result the school house and the church must work together. There must be Bibles in the schools that are to train teachers among this people, and there must be Christian men and women in them who both teach and practice religion."[41]

Some of the AMA teachers were ministers; many of the Black ministers in the South also taught in either the common (public) or AMA schools.

During the winter term problems with discipline continued to distress Ethel. She wrote again to her mother:

Black Congregational Church, Lexington, KY, attended by Ethel Applebee and other teachers, 1920-21.
EVA Collection

Ethel Applebee's Sunday School pupil, Lexington, KY. EVA Collection

I have one new pupil, making 34 or 35, don't know which, but it is enough. They are different from white children. When you think you are giving them a great scolding they usually go into gales of laughter. (Could it be my New England accent?) If you lose your temper you may as well pack your trunk, for they get the sulks or get more noisy than ever. About all you can do is be "firm," as you would say, and keep a twinkle in your eye.

Hope the boys will get along somehow. Hope you are able to make your dress. You haven't mentioned your eyes, so suppose they must be well as ever, as they were last fall. I wrote Mrs. Baldwin some weeks ago.

Love to all,

Ethel

Girls Basketball Team, Chandler Normal School, Lexington, KY, 1920-21.
EVA Collection

Chapter Seven - Ostracized and Celebrated

The teacher's salary at Chandler Normal School was $1,000 a year, or approximately $25 a week, with room and board provided.[42] The small salary did not allow for luxuries, and very little could be put away for the anticipated trip home for the summer. The girls learned how to be frugal, however. They had brought most of the clothes they needed with them, and only shopped when they found good sales. One such sale was a "fire and water sale." A fire in Lexington had destroyed a men's clothing store, two of the best department stores, and a smaller clothing store. Evidently the fire sale drew such crowds of people that a police guard had to be called in.

"They are having more sales this week," Ethel wrote. *"Am going down to see what I can find. Want to get a middy suit for school if I can."* She continued, *"Most of us hadn't much money to spend as haven't been paid this month's salary yet, but we all bought a few things. Shoes are awful high here, $10, $12, or even $18. But by looking around I finally got some decent looking oxfords for $4.98. Also got me a suit."*

After sending money home on occasion, and giving to the small black Congregational Church which she attended, Ethel was often low on funds. She mentioned this in one of her letters after Christmas: *Had a nice letter from Celia Smith, and a notice from Mr. Stover, telling of the $450 to be raised before Conference. Seems to me I do* *nothing but give away money this year. Hope I won't have to walk home."*

Ethel also dutifully sent her mother gifts from time to time. Mrs. Applebee's birthday was February 22, and Ethel got a good buy on a set of silverware at the fire and water sale. She wrote in January: *"I didn't get you any more stockings but perhaps you have bought some with the money I sent. I did get you something that will be for your birthday present, not to wear, for I can't seem to fit you. But it is something you have wanted for the house for a long time, and it, or they, are the real things."*

The stockings that Ethel had sent her mother at Christmas did not fit and her mother returned them to Ethel. In her letter of January 13 Ethel wrote:

"Got your letter, the stockings and the Bucksport Enter-prise, which have just finished reading. Will try to find you another pair of stockings. Have kept those for myself as needed some and they fit me all right. Since don't wear heavy underwear they are nice to keep the legs warm. Am sending a little present and will see about the stockings later. Glad you like the silver."

Doubt as to whether Chandler School would continue to receive support from donors was intimated in one of Ethel's letters during the winter. She wrote:

We expect some men from New York on February 3rd to visit school. Don't know yet whether school will open next year or not. The $7,100 which was to be raised by the alumni *and friends of the school seems to be hard to get and if it doesn't come in by May there will be no hope, we fear. None of us will know about jobs for next year, so we are all on the fence. We will start for home some time during the first week of June.*

If the rejection by the White people of the South affected Ethel and her friends, they did not let it be known. They enjoyed the friendship of the Colored teachers of Chandler, and also of Negro guests who came to visit the school during the winter. She wrote again in January:

We were invited out Sunday to the home of one of the Colored teachers. We went about 5 o'clock and had supper and spent the evening there until about 9:30.

On Friday there was a man here to speak in the interest of the school. A Colored minister from New Orleans. He was full of fun and could sing and recite. He spoke in the school chapel in the evening, then we had all the teachers over here. We talked, sang, and ate fudge till midnight. He left on Saturday morning."

In spite of the behavior problems Ethel encountered, there were a few of her students of whom she was especially fond. She wrote home about one of them in the following letter:

One of my boys, Harry Lee, reminds me of Sylvan when he has a sulky spell. I had to keep him after school one night when they were to play basketball, so that made him late for practice. The next morning I talked with him but he told me he "wasn't going to play anyway; they didn't need him; enough fellows trying to get his place; was going to give up his suit," etc. I told him I didn't believe him but he was sort of sulky all morning, but got thawed out a little after a while. Two mornings afterward he came in all agrin and said,

"Oh, Miss Applebee, I heard something good last night. I wouldn't give up playing for anything." Seems the coach told them they were to go to Virginia in February to play a team there. If they do, they will be gone several days. I called him down to my desk and asked him how he was going to get his suit back. He looked sort of blank and then he said, "Aw, I got to have a bigger one anyway." I told him that he wouldn't want to go without one. He went off grinning but he didn't want me to have the best of the bargain, so pretty soon he came down the aisle with his thumbs in his vest and still grinning he said, "Oh, I wouldn't play. I would just go as utility man." Of course we both were laughing by that time, and he was real decent all day.

We teachers didn't practice basketball this past week as one had to be away, and I had this bad cold, but expect we will one night this week. It is lovely outside, men stand around on street corners, basking in the sun. Well, I guess this will do for now, so goodbye. Love to all. Ethel

Under some circumstances the Negroes, as well as the Whites of the South, utterly, coldly spurned these White teachers from the North who had come to aid them. The history of the American Missionary Association reveals that after the Civil War thousands of teachers from New England, Indiana, Minnesota and other states had responded to the call for help in educating the Negro. Some of their experiences were less than pleasant.[43] There was one instance in which Ethel was totally rejected by one of her students, one from whom she least expected it.

It happened when one day she missed Robert Jackson from class, and the next day, and the next. Robert had been arriving early so she could tutor him in arithmetic. None of her other pupils seemed to know the reason for Robert's absence. Seeing his older sister in the hallway one day, Ethel inquired as to where Robert was and why he had not been in school. She was told he was in jail. On further inquiry Ethel found that he had stolen fifty dollars, had been caught, and that was why he was not in school. When he did not show up for more than a week, she decided to visit him. She had high hopes for Robert; there seemed to be higher than average intelligence in this handsome young man.

Ethel further discovered that Robert was actually on a juvenile farm for delinquent boys on the edge of town. She could get there by trolley. One afternoon she boarded the trolley near the school and headed out to visit Robert.

The building was an old, dilapidated building. At the top of the worn steps she pushed open the heavy wooden door. A grim-faced officer in a rumpled uniform sat at an old desk, reading a newspaper. When she asked to see Robert Jackson he gave her a sneering look of disapproval, and slowly led her down the hall to a square plain room where he told her to wait. There was an old battered table in the center and two rickety chairs. Ethel took one of the chairs which faced the door, while the officer went to get Robert.

Robert shuffled in behind the officer, handcuffed and sullen. When he saw his teacher his eyes opened wide and the semblance of his old smile appeared fleetingly. He sat in the other chair; the officer stood in the hallway outside the door, watching them.

Ethel told Robert about events in school, the baseball team, the work he had missed, and that she had missed him and hoped he would be back soon. He made no reply. The visit lasted about half an hour. Ethel was glad she had gone to see Robert. She wondered, did he know she cared about him? Did he hear what she said about making something of his life? On the way home she resolved to visit him again.

A few weeks later when Robert still had not returned to school, Ethel took the trolley to visit him the second time. The grim officer again admitted her, but there was cold hostility in his eyes, as if to say, "Why have you come again?" Ethel sat down in the same room to wait. When Robert walked in, again handcuffed, she sensed something had changed. There was no smile. He refused to look at her, keeping his eyes on the floor. He would not speak. He sat sideways on the chair, his head down, with his elbows on the table and his hands shielding his face from her. No matter what she said he made no response. It suddenly struck her, what she had been told was true! A Black man in the South does not dare associate, nor make friends, with a White woman.

Ethel realized she must leave immediately. As she signed out at the desk the jailer muttered under his breath, "If you teachers from the North were as smart as you think you are, you'd stayed home where you belong. We in the South know how to handle these Niggers, and we don't need your help."

A cold rainy drizzle wet her face and mingled with her tears as she almost ran to the trolley stop. Ethel was appalled. She had never heard such ugly words. She was filled with feelings of chagrin, hurt and anger...chagrined that she had unwittingly placed Robert in such a precarious position, hurt that he had spurned her who only wanted to be his friend, and angry at the surly jailer telling her she wasn't wanted in the South. But most of all she was shocked at the terrible discrimination by Whites against the Blacks.

She looked at the math book in her hand that she had meant to leave with Robert. He was not to be blamed for his attitude toward her. Now she understood he had been scared, very scared. A smile, a look of recognition, could get him a brutal beating, or worse.[44] (Lynchings, she remembered, were not uncommon in the South.) This awful hatred and animosity toward the Black race pervaded the very air. That, she now knew, was what made the South so different from the North.

Ethel Valentine Applebee, Seventh and Eighth Grade Teacher at Chandler Normal School, Lexington, KY, 1920-21.
EVA Collection

But not so at Chandler School. Here was friendly territory, and the Black children knew it. Here no one threatened them for having a White teacher friend. Here they were valued, encouraged, loved. But evidently other inmates at the juvenile institution, and no doubt the officer as well, had made it painfully clear to Robert that he would be in major trouble if he so much as spoke to his White teacher. With all her heart she hated this racism and vowed never to let it be a part of her. A love for her unfortunate Negro students in her classes who were obliged to live under such prejudice swept over her. A longing for her beloved northern homeland brought the tears. She arrived home during the supper hour, cold, wet, and discouraged. She went quietly up the staircase to her room, lay on the bed and cried.

The three northern teachers appreciated the gracious hospitality of Mr. and Mrs. Werking. They affectionately called Mr. Werking "Fessor," and Mrs. Werking was a second mother. The day after her birthday Ethel wrote about the grand party Mrs. Werking held for her:

February 13, 1921

Dear Mama,

Your letter written the 3rd came first of the week. I didn't send the box until Saturday the 5th, so of course you hadn't received it then, but you probably have it by this time.

My suit is green wool jersey rimmed with black buttons. I got enough chiffon at the sale to make me a waist and the girls gave me a green camisole (undergarment) to wear under it.

You know they give everyone a party for their birthday, so last night was my turn. Will send you some pictures of the affair. The decorations were all red and white. Crepe paper and candles, and Mr. Werking arranged the lights over the table so they are red and white. In the center was a nice white birthday cake. At every place was a little pasteboard basket filled with candy hearts and on the outside were little cupids. On the curtains were pinned red hearts and cupids. On the back of my chair was a large red and white bow, and at my place a huge stick of candy tied with red ribbon. And there were two packages wrapped in red. I opened one and found a blue camisole and opened the other to find a green one. The Colored teacher I am always writing about gave me a lovely white rose with a little spray of green with it. It is blooming here in the crack of the window to keep it fresh.

Mama, I can't believe I am 28 years old!

Went to town again. It is lovely and sunny today. Had to take off our coats and carry them on our arms on the way home from church. Yesterday was cold and rainy, so that one had to keep hustling to keep warm enough, so you see it is very changeable here.

Hope the boys are getting along well. Seems sort of dangerous for Vinal to work at night like that. S'pose Sylvan had a birthday too. I forgot about it until I was in school the other morning and wrote the date, February 10. Guess this is all.

Love, Ethel

Ethel's mother had given her the middle name of Valentine because she was born near Valentine's Day. She grew up making that her own special personal holiday. Ethel's class surprised their teacher by celebrating her birthday in their room one afternoon. Her letter of February 20th describes that occasion.

Dear Madam,

Yours of recent date at hand and contents noted, also the bundle of Enterprise newspapers. Our letters seem to be sort of crossed, as you get my answer before you write yours, but no matter. I intend to write every Sunday, if it kills me.

I told you about my party. I must tell you about my Valentine. Each classroom had Valentine boxes. I decided mine would be opened just before noon. When school opened that afternoon two of my biggest boys were late. It sort of worried me, as it is against all rules to be late after lunch. Then we have chorus that first period, and as Mrs. Werking plays for that she of course noticed that they were late. I asked one of them after they got back to my room where they had been, but he would not say.

Later in the afternoon I saw the other fellow put something on my desk but I thought at first it was a book, but later I looked and there lay a great big red envelope addressed to me. I opened it as I realized they expected me to, and inside was the cutest Valentine. A little girl sat in a hammock and beside her a little boy with a bunch of roses. They were fastened together so that when you pull the roses the boy swings the girl in the hammock.

It began to snow here sometime during Friday night and we had a real home snow storm all day yesterday. This morning there was about five inches, the most we have had, but it has stopped and is warmer today. It will be sloppy and muddy now for two or three days, then summer will be here again.

I sewed some yesterday, making up a new blue waist to go with my old blue suit. Hope to get a little more done this week as we have the 22nd for a holiday.

I must quit. They are yelling for me to come help get supper.

Love to all, Ethel

P.S. Glad you are pleased with the silver. I received the Valentines and birthday card from Mrs. Buck.

Chapter Eight - Trip to Mammoth Cave

Weary of winter and of teaching, Ethel, Sara, Lena, and Laura Carroll planned a trip for the upcoming Easter vacation. They had heard about the fabulous Mammoth Cave of Kentucky. Ethel had picked up a little book in the school library one day, entitled *Mammoth Cave, Kentucky*, written and published by John Thompson in 1909, describing the caverns.[45] None of the girls had ever seen underground caverns and since it was a rather inexpensive trip, they decided to visit the famous cave.

They took the Louisville and Nashville train out of Lexington on a Friday morning, headed for Louisville, and then boarded a trolley that would take them the nine additional miles to Mammoth Cave.

Ethel carried the little book with her on the trip, and while on the train to Louisville entertained the other girls by reading an excerpt:

"Wonderful Mammoth Cave! Wonderful it surely is, grand, weird and yet strangely fascinating. The realm of perpetual silence and everlasting night. Undoubtedly the greatest natural wonder in the western world. Human intellect is unable to realize or estimate the time required by the Almighty Architect of the universe to chisel out this gigantic cavern. The brain reels when one tries to fathom some of the mysteries to be seen on every hand—pits, domes, hills, valleys, pools and rivers are to be found in this strange place, all shrouded in Stygian darkness. This, the largest of all caves, is situated in Edmonson County, about ninety miles south of Louisville, near the main line of the Louisville and Nashville Railroad. It is claimed that about one hundred and fifty-two miles of avenues have been explored; but the tourist visiting the cave only sees those parts that are most easy of access...

"Volumes could be written about this remarkable cave region of Kentucky, embracing four or five counties where hundreds of caves are situated... In the Great Salt Cave some of the rocks are worn smooth where people have passed to and fro wandering about in this underground world long years before the white man ever set foot on this continent. Who knows but that perhaps the red man visited these caves out of curiosity as we of the twentieth century are doing? Although it is more likely that the caves were used as places of refuge when tribes were at war with one another. An occasional flint arrow or spear point can even to this day be found by diligent search around the entrance of some of the caves. Human bones are occasionally unearthed in some of the caves, testifying that many an unfortunate being has met his death in the early days when the outlaw and Indian roamed through this country...

"Mammoth Cave was first discovered by the white man in the year 1809. In 1837 it was opened to the public."

The Chandler teachers enjoyed their vacation trip immensely. Ethel wrote a long letter on April 1, describing Mammoth Cave, as well as their extended trip over to Hodgenville to visit the birthplace of Abraham Lincoln and the Lincoln Memorial. Wanting to share it,

Mabel Applebee, her mother, took it down to the editorial offices of the *Bucksport Enterprise*, hometown newspaper, which published it April 12 under the headline, "Miss Ethel Applebee Writes of Her Trip to Mammouth Cave." The article read: "Mrs. Charles Applebee has recently received a letter from her daughter, Miss Ethel Applebee, who is teaching this year at the Chandler Normal School in Lexington, Kentucky, which will be of interest to Miss Applebee's many friends here."

Lexington, Kentucky

April 1, 1921

Dear Mama:

Your card came today. Well, our vacation is about over and it's school again Monday morning. Guess I wrote you that we were going to Mammoth Cave for a trip. Well, we left here Friday morning and got to a place called Glasgow Junction that night at 5:30. Had to change cars at Louisville and had a little wait there. We spent the night at a common little hotel there, then in the morning went on to the Cave, a distance of 9 miles, but taking 50 minutes on the funny little train consisting of a queer little engine and one queer little car. When we reached the cave we found another hotel where we left our pocketbooks and clothes and changed into a brown drilling coat and bloomers. We took old shoes to wear in and also an old hat. After that we bought tickets for $2.10 which paid for the first tour, called Rt. #1. A man over sixty who has been there over thirty years was our guide. He *carried a gasoline lantern but the rest of us had a sort of torch or lantern with open blaze, one torch to a couple. To enter the cave we went down a lot of steps till we came to a sort of hollow in the ground.*

Will send you some pictures later. Have marked on the folder I sent Sylvan the places I have seen. Went down these steps till we came to a big hollow in the ground with a shelf like rock over the top from which was flowing a stream of water. When we were just at the entrance there was an iron grating gate which the guide unlocked for us to go in. There was such a draft that some of the lights went out, but we lighted up again. He then locked the gate and there we were!

Every place has its own name. For instance a big deep pit beside the path is named Bottomless Pit, a very narrow passage between rock walls is "Fat Man's Misery." You will see in the folder a picture of the boat ride on Echo River 360 feet below the surface of the earth. The river is 1/4 mile long. In another place there is quite a pool of water which is 30 ft. deep. This is known as the Dead Sea. They say there are fish there without eyes or even a place for an eye, a kind of cat-fish.

The last event was the Corkscrew of which I sent picture. Some job to climb those ladders, carry your lantern and not bump your head. The temperature is always the same, 54 degrees, but is warm enough for walking and climbing by torch light. We went in at nine o'clock and got out just before twelve.

There is another cave nearby and two more trips that could be taken in Mammoth. Lena and one girl took in the cave trip but the other girl, Sara, and I decided to go to Lincoln's birthplace instead as the cost was about the same, and none of us could afford both trips.

So we went back to the Junction and got the Saturday afternoon train to Elizabethtown, changed there for Hodgenville, which place we reached about 7:30. There was a very good little hotel there, and we had a hot bath and a good night's sleep, then spent Sunday seeing the town and the Lincoln Memorial. It is on the Lincoln Farm 3 miles from the village. We went to church in the morning, then after dinner we got a fellow with a girl and a Ford to drive us out, then back to Elizabethtown where we joined the other girls and we all went on to Louisville and spent the night at a YWCA place. We arrived home about 7:30 Wednesday night."
More later. Love, Ethel

P.S. I was sick with my stomach all day but got along without puking till I got home, then just let her go at frequent intervals till 1:30 in the morning. Yesterday, Thursday, I spent in bed and ate nothing and chewed it fine.

Today I got up, ate a little toast for breakfast, got dressed, had a bath and shampoo, ate toast for lunch with hot milk and a few strawberries without the shortcake, have been *out most all afternoon, bought a ukulele which I hope to be able to learn something about, but it just about takes the skin off a fellow's fingers to play it. Ate a good big dinner and now feel first rate, except for pain in my back caused by writing such a long letter. Hope you will be able to read it, something seems to ail my ink. Well, I don't write very often, but when I do you must admit they are long ones at least. Tell Mrs. Buck I got her Easter card. Better let her read this letter for I can't write many more to equal it.*

Lovingly, Ethel

Lincoln Memorial, Hodgenville, KY, visited by Ethel Applebee and Friends.
EVA Collection

**Brothers of Ethel Applebee: Sylvan, Vinal, and Clarence Apple-
bee.**
EVA Collection

Chapter Nine - Homesickness and Howard

It was late April. The school year was swiftly passing; spring was in full bloom. Ethel sat in her room late on a Sunday afternoon watching the sun go down. Her own room in Bucksport also looked westward. She was thinking of the year past, but also thinking ahead

**Francis W. Applebee, youngest
brother of Ethel Applebee.
EVA Collection**

to the trip home and to the summer and what might lie beyond. As she picked up her pen to write to her Mother once again, a wave of nostalgia swept over her, and for the first time since she came to Chandler tears of homesickness overflowed. She lay her head on the desk and wept. Dear Mother, she had been so faithful to write throughout the year. She had moved to Bucksport to be near Ethel, taking that job as matron at the seminary. Papa and Sylvan were running the farm in Enfield; oldest brother Clarence came home from the war with an eye injury and was living in Augusta with his new wife, Emma.

Vinal was the handsome outgoing brother with the dark hair and winsome smile, crazy about cars, who had set up a Chevrolet dealership in Enfield. Francis, youngest brother, was tall, with blond wavy hair, blue eyes and square jaw. He was the brother who most resembled Ethel.

She wished she had Francis's artistic talent. She loved the pencil drawings he sent. Outspoken, frugal, simple, bound by duty before pleasure, these were her people. She longed so much for home and family that afternoon.

She had to admit, too, that she missed Maine's pine trees, the white birch, the clear blue lakes, the pounding surf on the rockbound coast, and even the distinctive Maine accent that people in the South ridiculed. She would always be a Maine girl.

If she went back to Maine this summer what would she do? Probably she could get a teaching position near Bucksport if she did not return to Chandler. Little did she know then that very shortly events would transpire that would change her life forever.

Ethel knew that her position at Chandler was somewhat uncertain, with donations barely coming in. She would like to stay. She had made such good friends. How dear Mrs. Werking and the Professor had become—like second parents, caring for these Northern girls with their big hearts, guiding them with high ideals, nurturing them, loving them. Lena would like to stay at Chandler. Sara, the youngest of the four from the North, had become like a sister, too. Her cheerfulness and sweet manner had often calmed the storms of frustration that Ethel had experienced many days in the classroom.

Ethel had learned to love her children. Dear, unruly, loud, rambunctious children. How well they had done in the speaking contests! She saw their amazing musical talent. She loved to hear the voices of the glee club in chapel. Some of the smaller ones, with twinkling dark eyes, called her "Miss Apple." Those big boys, taller than she, finally learning their multiplication tables and parts of speech, had also made her proud.

And Robert. Unforgettable Robert. Something about this dark handsome lad had captured her heart. She had done her best to work patiently with him, for she saw underneath the rough exterior a tenderness, a sensitivity that was appealing. What had become of him? Would she ever see him again?

Maggie and Laura, the Negro teachers, also had become her good friends. They had so warmly accepted these girls with the "foreign" accent. They had laughed together, borne their school trials together, played games, popped popcorn, and pulled taffy on many a Sunday evening. In the midst of ostracization by the White people of the South, they had eased the pain of discrimination. They, too, were a part of the Chandler family that she loved. Ethel picked up her pen, dipped it in her ink well, and started to write. She didn't feel like writing a long letter tonight. This would be short:

Dear Mama,

Don't know just when I shall get home. Have had a fine time here this year but haven't saved much and you see there are only eight pay days instead of nine as at home.

It's worth a great deal to have had a chance like this, though. Hope I will be able to stand the heat all right. If I do, I shall call it a very good year indeed. The high school assistant is from Wisconsin. I'd like to go there with her, then down the Great Lakes by boat and home that way, but don't know. If we go the other way we will go to see Washington, D. C., and visit Congress if it is in session. Then may go on to New York to see the sights. Think after that I will have to look for a job for part of the summer anyway. Doesn't seem to be much to write about, so guess I will stop. Only six more weeks of school and two more pay days. The AMA does forward money for fare home.

Hope you are over your sick spell and that you may be able to use the skirt. How are the boys? Love to all. Write soon. Ethel.

P.S. Have you heard from Clarence? His business of tombstone engraving must be pretty dull if people no longer need grave stones. I thought that was a sure kind of business.

As Ethel finished the letter and placed the screw top on her ink bottle a soft tap came on the door.

"Ethel, Ethel, are you still up? I hope I'm not disturbing you."

"Oh yes, I'm still up. Just completed a letter to Mama. Come in." Ethel grabbed the damp handkerchief that lay on her desk and wiped her tearstained face.

"Ethel, you've been crying. What's the matter, dear?"

117

Sara was always so kind. She put her arms around her friend.

"Just a case of homesickness, I guess. Got to thinking about home. Too much Maine blood in me. There is so much of a difference between the North and the South. Guess I'll never fit in here." She dropped her head. "I don't know that I want to, either. How about you, Sara?" She looked at Sara quizzically. "What will you do next year if Chandler closes?" [46]

"Well, I really don't believe it will close. I plan to come back, and Lena does too, I expect. And of course you will be back with us. It wouldn't be Chandler without you, Ethel.

"I really came in to ask you something. It's just an idea that has been buzzing around in my head. How about you coming home with me for the summer? There's plenty of room at my home, and mother would love you. I know where we can get good summer jobs up in Yarmouth. Wouldn't that be fun? Besides that, you know I have a handsome brother not spoken for. Perhaps that would appeal to you?"

Ethel laughed. "Well, there certainly aren't any prospects in Kentucky. The White men won't look at us twice when they hear our Maine talk. I think when they hear we're teachers at Chandler they must think we are really strange. I never thought I was that bad looking! And you and Lena haven't had a bite either! That surprises me, for Lena was a real flirt in high school."

"Well, think it over, Ethel, and let me know. We could plan to stop in Washington if you like, and maybe even New York if our money holds out. Why don't you sleep on it? You look very tired."

Sara told her goodnight, hugged her, and slipped out, and Ethel got ready for bed. She suddenly realized how weary she was.

The next evening it was Ethel who tapped on Sara's door.

Ethel blurted out, "You didn't tell me his name, Sara. What's his name?"

"Whose name?" replied Sara innocently, knowing full well what Ethel meant.

"Why your brother's. If I am going to meet this man I want to know his name!"

"So you are going home with me, Ethel? How wonderful, simply wonderful. I'll write mother that you're coming. I'm so glad. It's going to be a great summer."

"Are you going to tell me his name?" Ethel was sounding exasperated.

"Oh, his name is Howard, and he's 27. You see, he's just the right age for you."

Ethel liked the name. Howard Leighton. As she walked back into her room she said to herself, "I wonder if she has a picture of him? Maybe I'll ask tomorrow, if I can get up my courage."

The heavy workload, giving exams, preparing the children for their final speech contest and the commencement program kept the teachers extremely busy. Ethel was not able to keep her faithful promise to write to her mother every week. Besides, there was something else, or someone else, on her mind.

**Howard Mayberry Leighton, U.S. Army photo, 1918.
EVA Collection**

When she mustered up her courage a few days later Ethel asked Sara if she had a picture of her brother. Sara replied, "I have been waiting for you to ask. I'll bring it to you this evening."

Ethel could hardly wait to get a glimpse of Howard. Ethel slipped up to her room soon after supper that evening to plan a few lessons and to sew, hoping that Sara would see her door open and come in with the picture. She had to wait until Sara helped clear the table and put things away in the kitchen, and finally she heard her come upstairs and go into her room. In a few minutes Sara came in and she handed Ethel a small photo. It was a small framed picture of a young man in Army uniform.

He was quite handsome, with a pleasant but serious face. Curiosity got the best of Ethel.

"How tall is he? What color are his eyes? His hair? What's he like to do? I really don't know much about your family, Sara."

Sara took the little rocker beside the window. "Howard is the oldest in the family and there are seven of us," she began. "We live on a farm in Cumberland Center. In 1918 Howard was drafted into the Cavalry of the Army and was sent to France. Almost as soon as he arrived the Armistice was signed, so he didn't have to stay. After he came home he wanted to try landscaping; trees and bushes have always been his great love. So he accepted a job with a landscape company in Maryland.

"He only got to stay a short while because Father became very ill and Mother called for him to come home and run the farm. Our father passed away in February a year ago. We have 75 acres. My brother

Ed is 25 and helps on the farm too. We have two younger brothers, Philip, who is 12 and Nathaniel, 6. We lost a brother, Wilfred, last December in an automobile accident.

"Oh, I'm sorry... Do you have any sisters?"

"I have two sisters. Ethel is one year younger than me. She is 21. Mabel is 19. Can you believe they are both shorter than me? We also have a number of cows, horses, chickens and pigs.

"On Sundays we all attend the Congregational Church in Cumberland Center.

Congregational Church, Cumberland Center, Maine.
EVA Collection

"As for Howard's looks, I think you'll find him nice looking. Light brown hair, blue eyes, about 5'8" with a nice build. He's very quiet, though. You'll have to get him to talk. And as I said, he's crazy about plants and bushes and trees, like our father—knows all about them. He's been like that ever since he was very small. Mother says when he was just a little boy he loved to look at the garden and plant catalogues that came in the mail. I think he cut his teeth on them!" Sara arose to leave.

Mmmm…A handsome farmer, quiet, intelligent, hard worker and probably very nice…oh, I can hardly wait to meet him, mused Ethel as she said goodnight to Sara, holding the photo of Howard tightly in her hand.

Chapter Ten - Closing Activities

During the month of May the teachers were busy with final exams and preparing the children for Anniversary Week early in June. The Home Economics Department students under Sara's guidance sewed garments and fancy articles for display and prizes. The Glee Club practiced overtime, anticipating the musical numbers they were scheduled to perform. Mrs. Werking worked with the soloists as they learned music and words to their special pieces, accompanying the all-school chorus. Ethel listened to speeches and coached her students for their presentations. Lena trained children to perfect their Palmer penmanship. A prize would be awarded to the student showing the most improvement in that department as well.

Commencement would follow, and finally the Demorest Gold Medal Speaking Contest. The Normal School Department of 20 pupils strived to complete all requirements for certificates leading to graduation. Sara helped these students fill out applications for teaching positions in Negro schools of the South, hoping they would get placements by fall. Mr. and Mrs. Werking coordinated all of the week's activities from May 28 through June 4. Mrs. Werking also planned the refreshments for the Open House for parents on Friday, May 28th. The program and activities went extremely well, and faculty, parents, and students were pleased with progress made and awards earned.

The Lexington Leader, the town weekly, the next day reported on the closing week of activities at Chandler. Mr. Werking went into town and picked up a copy of the paper for each of the teachers. School was over. No more lessons to plan, no more discipline to administer, no more rank cards to fill out. The teachers relaxed on the veranda that afternoon and enjoyed reading and discussing the newspaper article. The headline read:

CLOSE OF YEAR ANNIVERSARY WEEK OF CHANDLER NORMAL SCHOOL[47]

Interesting Exercises Showing the Progress Made by this Excellent Institution for the Education of the Colored Race

"Chandler Normal School's Anniversary Week was opened by the Open House on Friday. Visitors to the school throughout the forenoon were entertained by the display of work accomplished by the young people in various rooms. A spelling contest resulted in awarding a year's tuition to a student in the eighth grade. At one o'clock the school gathered in the chapel to hear the closing rhetorical exercises of the eighth grade. Four young essayists spoke on historical subjects. The program was supplemented by four speakers from the seventh grade. The music interspersed with the speeches consisted almost entirely of piano selections.

"On Monday morning the Glee Club presented a cantata, 'The Musical Enthusiast.' The second part of the program was a piano recital by the pupils of the music department which showed a degree of excellence in musical instruction bringing down the highest praise upon the music teacher. The musical selections included piano solo, Mozart Sonata No. 9, and a violin rendering of the sweet old melody, Old Folks at Home, which everyone very much enjoyed.

"The exercises in the chapel on Tuesday were opened by 'Nearer My God To Thee,' followed by the Scholarship Declamation contest by the young women of the Normal Department which showed thorough and conscientious training on the part of the instructors.

"'My Old Kentucky Home' was rendered very beautifully and received an encore. The sympathetic rendering of Dickens' pathetic 'Child's Dream of a Star' showed the speaker to be one of unusually clear understanding and won for her second prize, a half year's tuition. 'Lady Yeardley's Guest' won first prize, a year's tuition, and enthusiastic applause. A vocal solo, 'The Holy City,' was liked so well as to receive a recall. An eight hand piano selection closed that portion of the program."

The newspaper article continued by reporting that there were other awards for sewing, improvement in penmanship and for perfect attendance, and listed the names of those who had first and second ranking in grades four through eleven.

The contest that most interested Ethel took place on Wednesday of the last week of school at Chandler. The *Lexington Leader* also reported that event:

"A small but very appreciative audience assembled to listen to the Demorest Gold Medal Speaking Contest on Wednesday.[48] The contestants were those who had been awarded silver medals during the past year. These appeared in the order in which they had won. They each delivered their speeches without a fault and waited for the verdict as to the winner which came after the address of the day was delivered by a lawyer of Lexington. His subject was 'The Positive Side of Temperance as Distinguished from its Purely Negative Aspect.'

"Mr. Werking, Director of the school, then presented the gold medal to the winning contestant, who had rendered a most happy and eloquent address, highly appreciated by the audience. The morning concluded with two selections from the Glee Club, a vocal solo and a piano trio, all very well received."

Thursday saw the awarding of twenty Teaching Certificates to eager graduates of the Normal Department. This was the climax of the year. The purpose of Chandler Normal School was to prepare students to teach the Negro children of the South. Obviously there was great satisfaction in the hearts of the director and staff that once again that goal had been accomplished.

Ethel folded the newspaper and looked soberly out across the beautiful campus of Chandler.

How happy the graduates had looked as they trooped triumphantly in their black robes out of the chapel and down the wide marble steps, coveted diploma in hand. Many had already received replies to their applications and had been appointed to teach in public schools, confirming that Chandler graduates were well qualified and accepted.

She remembered that she had come to Chandler to assist in a worthy cause—teaching the underprivileged so they might lift their race through education. She was especially proud of her students this day as she saw so many of them receive awards. They had done so much better than she had expected after the rough beginning. Some of her trouble makers had settled down to become good students; they had finally set their minds to learning, and even the slowest showed vast improvement.

Campus of Chandler Normal School, Lexington, KY.
EVA Collection

It all recalled to Ethel's mind that wonderful day in Bucksport when she herself had walked across the platform at East Maine Conference Seminary in 1911 to receive her Normal School diploma and begin her teaching career. She thought of Wellington. If only he could be here. She knew he would have been pleased.

And somewhere along the way her pupils had learned to appreciate the Northern young lady with that often-misunderstood accent who had come to teach them. Ethel felt well rewarded for the months she had spent here.

But it wasn't all work, Ethel reminisced. She and Lena, Sara, and Katherine had a lot of fun together, shopping, taking weekend trips or rides in the country. Most Sunday mornings they attended the little Congregational church which some of their pupils attended, and Sunday evenings were spent with the Colored teachers, singing around the piano and playing games. How she had enjoyed the trip to Mammoth Cave. She hoped that they would all be together again next year here at Chandler. Still, there hung in the back of her mind the face of that handsome Howard in Cumberland Center, Maine, and her coming visit to his home. (Ethel suspected Sara had written to him about her.) Her heart skipped a beat as she thought of meeting Howard. What would she say to him, he to her? Would he like her? What if it turned out that this was her last year of teaching? Was she ready for that? Or was she jumping ahead of herself? Maybe she was being foolish and presumptuous. Then again, she thought that maybe, just maybe, she might be willing to give up teaching if Howard turned out to be all she dreamed he'd be.

Chapter Eleven - Next Year's Appointments

The next day was spent cleaning rooms, packing trunks, saying goodbye to the staff and other teachers, getting ready for their departure for home on Monday morning. In the afternoon Mr. Werking drove to the train station to purchase their tickets. The teachers appreciated his many kindnesses to them.

At the breakfast table on Friday morning Mr. Werking asked all of the teachers to meet in his office at 11:00 a.m. They wondered if this was the time he would tell them whether Chandler would be open next year. Lena popped into Ethel's room.

"What do you think, Et? Are we fired or hired? Guess we'll soon find out."

"Yes, they certainly ought to let us know before we leave for home whether we'll be coming back next year."

Ethel, Lena, Sara and Katherine gathered with the two Colored teachers, Ella, Mattie and Laura, at the appointed time. Mr. Werking greeted them, smiling and relaxed. (That's a good sign, thought Ethel.) He asked the young ladies to be seated, and he took his place behind his big desk. His manner eased their apprehension considerably.

"You will be glad to know that I just yesterday received a telegram from the American Missionary Association in New York." He took the yellow telegram from his top desk drawer and read:

"'JUST RECEIVED DONATION FROM BENEFACTOR STOP CHANDLER WILL REMAIN OPEN NEXT YEAR STOP'"[49]

The Professor put the telegram back in the drawer and from a large brown envelope on top of his desk he removed several sheets of paper. He went on:

"AMA has been very pleased with the progress made by the students at Chandler this year. I commend each of you for a job well done. I received your next year's appointments a week or so ago from New York, but could not give them to you until I had the assurance that funds had come in to cover expenses for next year. So Ethel Applebee, Sara Leighton, Katherine Lewis, and Lena Spencer, each of you are hereby officially appointed as teachers to Chandler Normal School for the year 1921-1922. Congratulations." He shook hands with each of them as he handed them their official appointments.

The girls were overjoyed and hugged each other, laughing and smiling. Mr. Werking continued:

"I am very pleased to announce that you, Ella Ross, Mattie Smith, and Laura Carroll, have also been reappointed. Here are your official appointments as well. Congratulations to each of you." Broad smiles covered their faces, and hugs went around again.

Ethel wrote her mother a short letter that evening, telling of her plans for the summer:

Dear Mama,

We have finally heard that all of us teachers have been reappointed to Chandler for next year. We are relieved that someone has come forward with enough funds to keep the school open for at least another year.

I want to tell you too, that Sara Leighton, the teacher from Cumberland Center has invited me to come home with her for a week. She lives on a farm with her mother and brothers and sisters. She is very nice, and I am sure I will enjoy visiting with her family. So if this is all right with you I will plan to stop there for a week on my way home. That means I will be arriving in Bucksport about June 12. I will let you know exact time and date later. Lena will go on to Enfield to her parents' home. We all need to get jobs for the summer, and it could be that I will be working with Sara at a Y this summer. Will let you know later. Can't wait to see my family and home again.

Love, Ethel

Now that Ethel had her official appointment to teach at Chandler the following year, she pondered what she should pack to take home and what she should leave. She finally decided to take all of her good clothes, the ones she had purchased in Lexington and the ones she had made, and leave her older clothes at Chandler. If perchance she did not come back, they could be sold at Mrs. Werking's store. By the time she had everything packed there was no room for her beloved books. She hated leaving them, but knew they would be safe in her room. If she did not return, she was sure Sara or Lena would ship them to her. If she did come back to Lexington next year, of course she would need them.

It took two trips for Mr. Werking to drive the girls and their trunks to the railroad station on Monday morning. He first brought Ethel and her trunk to the station, and then returned for Sara and Lena and their things. Their bulky hat boxes took up most of the room.

By 10:30 Ethel, Sara, and Lena had boarded the train, headed for Maine and home.

The three Maine teachers took the Louisville & Nashville Railroad to Cincinnati where they transferred to the Baltimore and Ohio, which would eventually take them to Washington, D.C. This would be their first visit to the Nation's Capitol. While Ethel had always thought Maine, with its lakes and forests, and its rugged rockbound coast must be the most beautiful state of all, on that trip she discovered that there were comparable spots in many states. The girls were struck speechless as they viewed the high Appalachians of West Virginia, and breathless as the train inched around perilous mountain curves and plunged into valleys. Soon they were traveling up through the lovely tree-covered Blue Ridge mountains of Virginia. The train finally turned Northward over the flattened eastern terrain and crossed the Potomac River, into the Nation's Capitol. They were awestruck at the huge arched dome of Union Station; they felt like they were in a huge cavern. Their voices echoed as they endeavored to be heard above the din of the crowd. They walked toward the entrance and beyond saw the awesome Capitol dome. They never dreamed it would be so big!

133

Ethel had particularly wanted to visit Washington to see the newly completed Lincoln Memorial, which was to be dedicated the following year on Lincoln's birthday (and hers). She wanted to compare it with the memorial to Lincoln which she had seen in Hodgenville, Kentucky.

But first, they quickly agreed, they must visit the Capitol that loomed close by. They hurriedly walked the few short blocks.

The rotunda with its lofty dome was beyond description. The large paintings of historic moments in early American history and the marble statues of great personages of each state around the perimeter captivated their attention. They noted that Frances Willard, founder of the Woman's Christian Temperance Union, and of whom they had read many times, was the only woman honored with a statue in the rotunda. Realizing their time was limited, they hurried down the Mall to the Lincoln Memorial. The massive marble structure surrounded by 36 Doric columns took their breath away. In silence they climbed the wide steps leading to the main hall in which sat the huge statue of the sober Emancipator, surrounded by inscriptions of his Gettysburg Address and Second Inaugural Address. Here, as in the Capitol building, sightseers spoke only in whispers as if they were in a sacred place. From the high vantage point on the top step the teachers could view the Potomac River to their right, the pool reflecting the Washington Monument, and the Capitol beyond. They took pictures and lingered several minutes, and then, remembering they had a train to catch, took a cab back to Union Station.

Lincoln Memorial, Washington, D. C. visited by Ethel Applebee, 1921.
Author's Collection

They boarded the train, thankful that they had Pullman reservations. After a night's sleep they would arrive in Boston to board the ferry to Portland.

Knowing it was to be a long trip, the three friends were happy when the porter told them he would make up their berths about 9:00 p.m. The farewells at Chandler, their long ride from Lexington to Washington, and the sightseeing had exhausted them. They slept well, and in the morning had to wait only minutes before the train pulled into Boston South station. A redcap helped carry their luggage to a waiting taxi, which took them to the wharf, from where the ferry for Portland would soon depart. How good to see the ocean again, thought Ethel. She hadn't realized how much she had missed it! As she planted her feet on the gently rolling deck and breathed in the salty breezes, the strain of the past year dropped away from her shoulders. She thought of her beloved Maine, her Mother waiting there, and also of a certain young man whom she was most eager to meet.

Chapter Twelve - Ethel Meets the Leightons

After several hours the ferry moored in Portland harbor. As they waited for their luggage, Ethel turned to say goodbye to Lena and gave her a big hug. Lena was such a good friend. Together they had weathered many a storm, laughed and cried together, sharing their joys and triumphs as well as adventures. Now Lena would head north by train to Enfield where her parents were waiting for her.

"Goodbye, Et. I hope to see you next year. Don't fall in love too quickly. Please write to me. I'll miss you two." She gave Sara a hug, and Ethel another squeeze, waving as she followed the porter with her luggage to the waiting train that would take her north. Portland was a neat little city. From her enlarged perspective Ethel marveled that except for the train porters and red- caps there were so few black faces to be seen here.

Since Sara had written to inform her family the time of their arrival, the girls waited until one of her brothers, either Howard or Ed, would come to take them to the Leighton farm.

Ethel was admittedly nervous. She was about to meet Howard! It seemed hours ago that she had arisen and donned her bright blue dress with the red sash and red collar. She had carefully pinned her long wavy auburn hair up on top of her head in what people said was the most attractive fashion. Secretly she hoped Howard would find her appealing; from his picture he already appealed to her.

Presently a shining black Model T Ford touring car came along-side the curb near the bench on which Sara and Ethel were sitting. Ethel knew Howard immediately. Sara, surprised at the new car, ex-claimed:

"Howard! When did you get the new car? I expected you'd be driving the truck!"

Howard jumped out of the driver's seat with a big grin, doffed his cap to Ethel, picked up their two suitcases, and carefully piled them into the back seat. He would return later for the trunks, he said.

Ethel stood still, watching and waiting to be introduced. Sara fi-nally said, "Howard, this is Ethel, my friend from Chandler that I wrote you about. Ethel, this is my brother Howard."

Ethel reached out to shake his hand and liked his firm grip. His blue eyes met hers and held them for a brief moment, and Ethel thought she saw a flicker of admiration in them. Howard opened the car doors and Sara climbed in the back, forcing Ethel to sit in the front with Howard. Did Sara plan it that way? Ethel would ask her later! The drive out to the farm was along a bumpy dirt road.

Leighton Homestead, "Woodland Farm," Falmouth, Maine, built by Amos Leighton, grandfather of Howard M. Leighton.
EVA Collection

Sara asked again, "When did you get the car, Howard? I didn't expect this."

"I decided I'd better have something better than the farm truck to pick up two fine ladies from the South. Besides, mother wanted to go up to Yarmouth to Mabel's graduation yesterday, so I decided to buy this Ford. Glad you like it."

He paused, "You know, we lost the truck in Wilfred's accident last December." There was a trace of sadness in his voice. Ethel recalled Sara telling her about the loss of their brother, Wilfred. Coming home from a dance he and two other boys ran off a bridge and plunged into the river.[50]

After several miles Howard turned the car into a large yard, stopping in front of the long front veranda of the Leighton homestead.

He ran around to open the doors for Ethel and Sara. Standing in the doorway was Nina Leighton, a short, slightly stout woman of about forty-five whose warm smile made Ethel feel welcome immediately.

"Come in girls, I've been expecting you. Supper is about ready. I hope you are hungry."

Sara introduced Ethel to her mother, who grasped her hand with both of hers, and said, "I'm so pleased to meet you. Sara has written so much about you. Come in and make yourself at home."

Howard brought the suitcases in and took them up the winding stairs. His mother invited Ethel to come up to the bedroom to the right of the stairs that she would share with Sara during the visit. The ceiling of the room peaked above the bed. The bed was made up neatly with a heavy white crocheted coverlet. A washstand with pitcher and basin was in the corner, a wardrobe against the far wall. A multicolored handmade braided oval rug lay on the floor beside the high posted bed. Ethel could see the front yard and the large red barn from the dormer window, As soon as Mrs. Leighton went downstairs Ethel sank into the soft featherbed, relishing the moment. She thought, "I really like Howard. I like his sweet mother. I love it here. I feel so welcome." She washed her face and hands, powdered her nose, straightened her hair and went down to eat and meet the rest of the family.

Mrs. Leighton had set a large table in the dining/living room with white tablecloth and linen napkins. Both the dishes and the silverware were well worn. Ethel remembered that this home had been built by Sara's grandfather, and no doubt most of the furnishings had been handed down over the years. Ethel couldn't wait to plunge into a pile of those Maine mashed potatoes and the roast beef and gravy, the homegrown string beans, and fried chicken. One by one the children gathered at their places around the table. Mrs. Leighton sat at the head of the oval table, and Howard assumed the place that had no doubt been his father's, at the opposite end.

On one side of the table were Edward, who looked a little like Howard but was a couple of years younger, Philip, a quiet, blond boy of 12, and little Nathaniel, dark-haired and shy, about 6. On the other side of the table were the three sisters, Sara, Ethel, a working girl of about 21, and Mabel, who had just graduated from high school. (Ethel

Applebee, seated next to Howard, would ever after be called "Ethel number two," to distinguish her from sister Ethel.)

She wondered again if she had been seated next to Howard purposely! The conversation centered mostly about the girls' activities, especially those of Sara and Ethel at Chandler. Mabel was lively and witty; Ethel was quiet and thoughtful, Sara was the talker. Edward tried several times to change the subject to the farm and how the pigs and cows were doing. Howard didn't say a word.

After the last bite of apple pie Howard remembered he was to pick up the girls' trunks in Portland. He excused himself and as he started to leave he turned to Ethel.

"You girls better go with me. I have to have someone along who can identify your trunks." Ethel looked at Mrs. Leighton, who smiled approvingly. Ethel joined Sara and they went out to get in the Model T Ford with Howard.

Sara again quickly climbed into the back seat, leaving the front seat for Ethel. Riding beside him in the Model T along the country road into Portland, Ethel felt perfectly at ease with Howard. He was polite and courteous, and a good driver. It was clear that he was admired by his brothers and sisters and that his mother depended on him. It was also obvious that he was the man in charge of the farm, and very capable of running it. Ethel liked his gentle but strong manner. Her heart told her that he had special feelings for her by the way he looked at her, and his deference, helping her in and out of the car.

(Many years later Howard's younger brother, Philip, was to write to his niece in Maryland, "I think Howard and Ethel fell in love at first sight.")[51]

When Howard, Sara, and Ethel drove into the yard the girls had finished the dishes and the boys had milked the cows. The family was seated on the veranda steps, enjoying the fading daylight and watching the moon come up. Nathaniel tried to catch the lightning bugs that flitted about the yard. Having Sara home again was great. Sisters Ethel and Mabel talked about how pretty Ethel Applebee was and wondered if Howard at last had a real girl friend. The little brothers thought Ethel was fun. Mother Leighton hoped Howard had found his heart's desire. It had been hard for him the past year, to lose his father from a stroke, and then his brother Wilfred, only 23, in December. It had thrust upon Howard the burden of running the family farm, forcing him to give up his plans to go to Maryland and work in the landscape business.

Their habit of all turning in early suited Ethel just fine; tired from their trip and excited about meeting Howard, she bade them all good night.

The feather bed engulfed her but she couldn't sleep. Finally she climbed out and went to the window. The silver moon hung low and shed its white light over the barn, the meadow, and the trees beyond. And, Ethel thought, that same moon hangs over my home in Bucksport and over Chandler School in Lexington. She wondered if she would be going back there; she wondered what Mother would think when she told her about Howard. Kneeling there beside the window casement she breathed a prayer for Divine guidance in the future that lay unknown before her.

The grandfather clock at the foot of the stairs gonged two before Ethel drifted off to sleep.

**Nina Wagner and Edgar Barton Leighton,
parents of Howard M. Leighton.
EVA Collection**

Chapter Thirteen - Home Again

As Ethel fell into the farm routine, the days that followed were relaxing. Everyone got up early. Howard was milking cows before the sun was up; the smaller boys collected the eggs, Ethel and Mabel helped in the kitchen getting breakfast, Edward looked after the pigs and fed the horses. Ethel A. busied herself with a variety of tasks. Most often she helped in the kitchen, washing dishes and talking with Mother Leighton. She watched Mrs. Leighton, Mabel and Ethel make butter, and learned that the farm sold 100 pounds of butter a week, as well as dozens of eggs.

Several evenings Howard invited Ethel to go for a ride with him with the ruse that he had to borrow a tool at a neighbor's house, or to make arrangements for help with planting the acres of corn that would become silage for the cows that winter. She gladly accepted the rides, for it gave them time alone. Sara noted the shining eyes, the sweet smile that covered Ethel's face when she returned from these rides. She was so glad she had brought Ethel home with her.

One day Sara asked Howard to take her and Ethel the ten miles up the coast to Princess Point, the location of the summer hotel with a beautiful view of the ocean, where they applied for summer jobs. They were hired right away, and would be living there during the summer months, with Sundays off. They would begin working in two weeks.

Ethel had planned to go home for a few days and Howard offered to drive her to Bucksport. It was more than 100 miles, and since she already had her train ticket, Ethel insisted on taking the train home. But he could come up and get her, she said, when she returned to begin the summer job with Sara at Princess Point.

A few days later Ethel said goodbye to the Leighton family. With luggage piled into the rear seat of his Ford, Howard drove her to the Portland train station. After her trunk was taken by the red cap and she was about to board the train, Howard handed Ethel her small suitcase. "See you soon, sweetheart," he said softly. Surprised and pleased, for once Ethel didn't know what to say. But she surely would be back to this sweet man she was beginning to love more than she dared think.

On the train Ethel relaxed, glad to be headed toward Bucksport and home. She could smell the pine tree forests. As she saw the sturdily built Maine homes with their attached wood sheds and barns and the farm animals out to pasture, she thought how different this was from the South she had left behind. She caught glimpses of white caps dashing on the rocks, and the stands of white birch among the evergreen trees scattered in the woods beside the Penobscot River as the train turned northward. It was more beautiful than she remembered. It was so good to be back in Maine, her state. She looked forward to seeing her brothers, Sylvan, Vinal and Francis, all grown taller by now, she was sure. Ethel wondered how she should tell her mother about Howard. Very casually, she guessed. After all, they only met a week ago! But deep down Ethel knew things had moved beyond "casual." She was sure the deep feeling she had for Howard were akin to the feelings he had for her. This was a new experience; she must admit she had fallen head over heels in love.

Vinal picked her up at the train station in Bucksport, and soon she was seated in the kitchen while Mother prepared to put supper on the table. One by one the brothers entered the room: Vinal, in mechanic's uniform, with his black wavy hair slicked back, Francis, the athlete, baseball cap in hand and still in his baseball suit, grinning and saying, "We won another game. I pitched a shutout. That makes two in a row." Mother said Sylvan was still helping to run the farm in Enfield with his father. After they gathered around the table and said grace, Mother turned to Ethel.

"Tell us about Sara and her family. Does she have any brothers or sisters? Did you meet her mother and father?"

Here was the opening Ethel had hoped for, to tell about the Leighton family, and especially about Howard.

"Oh, yes, she has four brothers and two sisters. The older brothers are Howard and Ed, and the younger brothers are Philip and Nathaniel. They are only eleven and six. The sisters, Sara, Ethel and Mabel are between the boys. They live on a farm outside of Portland. Since his father died last year, Howard runs the farm with Ed's help. They made me feel very welcome, and I had a great time. Mrs. Leighton is very friendly and I helped her make butter. They sell 100 pounds a week![52] Howard just got a new Model T Ford and took me to the train station."

Something about the way Ethel's blue eyes lit up when she said Howard's name told Mrs. Applebee that this was more than a casual acquaintance. She asked discreetly, "How old are Ed and Howard?"

"Well, let me see. Howard is the oldest, a year younger than I, and Ed is two years younger than Howard. I think Ed is engaged to a Norwegian girl on the next farm, Ethel Peterson."

"That leaves Howard for you, Ethel," teased Francis mischievously. "Has he kissed you yet?"

Ethel blushed. "Please pass the peas," she asked, trying to regain her composure. "How are Papa and Sylvan? Got the corn planted yet? Are they coming up soon? I hope so. Haven't had but one letter from Papa all year. None from Sylvan."

Ethel and her mother were washing the supper dishes when Ethel said, "I've been appointed to teach at Chandler School again next year. Sara and Lena are going back too. It's been a great year, and we had a fine time. Good to feel that we contributed something to the Negro children. I wish you could have visited us, Mama. You would have enjoyed the children."

"Ethel, I'm proud of you. I would like to see Chandler School. But it is so far away. I've missed you, my dear. I appreciated all your letters. But the South is different, isn't it?"

"Very, very different, Mama. You wouldn't believe the prejudice. The white people don't approve of teachers from the North coming there, and most of the Negro parents would rather have teachers of their own race in the classrooms. Can't blame them. We talk so different sometimes the children laugh at us, like it is a foreign language.

Of course we found it hard to get used to their way of speaking too. So many expressions I couldn't understand."

"What will you do this summer?" It was a leading question.

"Well, as I said in my last letter, Sara and I have applied and been accepted to work at a summer hotel at Princess Point this summer in Yarmouth, about ten miles from where they live. I knew there would be nothing around here, so I took the job. I'll have to leave here in two weeks and be on the job by July 1."

She paused, and then said quietly, "Howard is coming up to get me and take Sara and me to Yarmouth. The hotel where we'll be working is quite beautiful, overlooking Casco Bay."

Mother knew her daughter Ethel very well. Her tone of voice was saying something that was not in the words. She guessed correctly that Ethel wanted her to meet Howard and approve of him.

"Well, I'd hoped I would get to meet him soon. You seem quite smitten with him, Ethel. Maybe it is about time you settled down, got married and had a family, like most girls your age." Mabel Applebee was not one for mincing her words.

There, I've told her, and she knows, thought Ethel. Can't see any reason why she wouldn't approve of Howard. I can't wait for them to meet. I hope Howard will like my family as much as I like his.

Ethel kept busy during the next two weeks. She unpacked her trunk, washed clothes, sewed uniforms and white aprons to wear on her new job, polished her oxfords. She picked buckets of blueberries and raspberries in the back meadow behind the house. She and her mother worked side by side canning and making jam, and once in a while a blueberry or rhubarb pie. Her mother was happy to have Ethel close again. Secretly she hoped that Ethel would meet and marry the "right" man and then settle down not far from home. Since she was an only daughter it was hard not to have her near by. At least Portland was not as far away as Lexington, Kentucky.

Howard made sure he had the directions to Ethel's home before he left Cumberland Center Sunday to drive up to Bucksport. He arrived late in the afternoon. Ethel had been watching for him from the swing in the front yard for more than an hour, and ran to the car when he drove in. The car was so shiny; she guessed he had been polishing it. How handsome Howard was, dressed in his Sunday best. Of course he wanted to make a good impression on Ethel's family. Mrs. Applebee greeted him cordially at the door as he came up the steps with Ethel, and invited him into the front parlor.

"You must be tired from such a long trip. Come in and rest. Would you like some iced tea?"

Howard was not talkative around strangers, but he smiled and said yes, he was tired, and yes, he would like some iced tea. When Mrs. Applebee came back with a tray of tea and sugar cookies he stood up and thanked her. Vinal came in, and the ice was broken, for conversation came easily to him. Howard seemed more at ease then. Vinal asked about the car and how long it took him to drive up from Portland, and how often he had to stop for gas.

Ethel was all packed and wanted to leave right away. But her mother insisted, since it was so late, that Howard stay overnight. After all, it was a seven hour drive and Howard was tired. Francis moved into Vinal's room and Howard was given Francis' room for the night. Howard seemed to appreciate Mrs. Applebee's thoughtfulness of his welfare, but Ethel wished that her mother had not been so insistent.

Both Ethel and Howard were up early the next morning, Monday, eager to start the trip by eight o'clock. Ethel made pancakes for Howard, spread with home-made blueberry jam. At the last minute her mother packed two jars of raspberry jam in a little box for Howard to take to his mother. Howard thanked her several times and shook her hand before they drove off. The thought occurred to Howard that possibly the next time he would drive to Bucksport it might be for a wedding. As Mrs. Applebee watched the two drive off she had the same thought.

When they arrived at Howard's home Sara was anxiously waiting, all packed and dressed. After a hasty late lunch they said goodbye to Mother Leighton and headed up to Yarmouth. The girls were to begin work the next day, July 1, 1921.

Chapter Fourteen - Romance at Princess Point

It was a busy but rewarding summer for both Sara and Ethel, and a needed change from the strenuous year at Chandler. They were assigned to kitchen and dining room duty which kept them busy eight hours a day. Sunday was their day off. Howard had asked Ethel if he could come to see her on Sunday afternoons. "Oh, yes, Howard, of course. I'd love to see you any time," she replied, hoping she hadn't sounded overly eager! She wanted to see him whenever she could, Sunday or any other day of the week. The week seemed to drag by; Ethel could scarcely wait for Sunday afternoon.[53]

As soon as church was over and he had eaten Sunday dinner with the family, Howard headed up to Princess Point. Ethel listened for that Model T Ford to pull onto the grounds and up the hill to where she waited on the lawn. Each week they took leisurely long drives up the coast, stopping at lookouts along the way, viewing the ocean and listening to the waves beating on the rocky shore. Ethel always dressed her prettiest for these excursions, usually in blue, her long wavy auburn hair swept up to the top of her head and falling long down her back. Howard liked it that way.

Their love blossomed. Ethel learned of Howard's heartaches and of his dreams. She learned of his great interest in flowers and plants when he would stop the car along the side of the road and climb down to look at wild flowers or blooming bush. He would even tell her the

Latin names of most of them, which astounded her. How did this farm boy have so much knowledge of these things? Plants and bushes were a passion with Howard. Walking in the woods he would pick a bunch of wildflowers for Ethel, presenting them to her as he said their Latin names. She loved him for that.

Ethel learned firsthand from him how his father had suffered a stroke while Howard was working for a landscape company in Maryland just a little over a year before. Mother had called him to come home to run the farm. His father died just two weeks after Howard arrived home, February 8, 1920.

On another day as they sat on a huge rock overlooking the ocean he told her how his younger brother, Wilfred, his partner on the farm, had gone to a dance one night the previous December with two other boys, and how coming home their truck had plunged off a bridge into the river, and that all three boys drowned. Howard told her, too, of

his dream that one day he would go back to Maryland to work at the landscape company, doing what he loved best. This appealed to Ethel; she could not exactly picture herself a farmer's wife.

He told her of his being drafted in 1918 into the Cavalry of the U.S. Army, and being sent to France. He considered himself lucky that he did

Yarmouth Academy, high school attended by Howard M. Leighton.
Author's Collection

not have to fight, as the war ended soon after he arrived.

One day he drove Ethel over to see the Yarmouth Academy, a large two-story square brick building, where he had attended high school. It made Ethel think of Chandler, and for a moment nostalgia swept over her as she wondered if she would be going back. Howard told her how he had walked the five miles each day to school and back, but he hadn't minded it, for on those long walks he had discovered so many interesting plants. It was not unusual for him to carry some of them home with him to preserve in his Herbarium album to show his botany teacher. Ethel loved the hours with Howard on those leisurely Sunday afternoons.

Ethel told Howard about Chandler, how and why she and Lena went to Lexington, and even about Wellington and his dream. She described the children and how she had taught them public speaking. He asked her to recite some of her favorite poems to him on one occasion, and she obliged with "The Children's Hour" and "Psalm of Life," both by her favorite poet, Henry Wadsworth Longfellow of Portland. He didn't know how in the world she could remember all those lines!

He enjoyed hearing of her trip to Mammoth Cave and to Washington D.C., and particularly of her visit to the Lincoln Memorial, for he had visited Washington in connection with his job at the nursery. Howard took note that she loved traveling and history. He wondered when he would travel to Washington again.

When he arrived one August Sunday in mid-afternoon Howard asked Ethel if she could prepare a picnic—he wanted to drive her up to Boothbay Harbor. Ethel went to the kitchen and packed them a lunch, sensing they would be gone for a while. Howard was very quiet as he drove, and both enjoyed the intimate silence of each other's presence. Ethel had a feeling that Howard had something special in mind.

They drove north on Route 1, through Brunswick, and turned down the road that led to Boothbay Harbor. Howard parked the car and hand in hand they walked out over the huge gray rocks overlooking the water. There were boats of all sizes coming and going, local fishermen bringing in their catches of the day, seagulls soaring lazily overhead. The waves gently lapped the rocks at their feet; the afternoon sun danced and played on the white caps. They opened the blanket and sat down to watch the view. To find someone who enjoyed these shores as she did filled Ethel's heart with joy. To be near Howard was to be at peace. He was so strong, and so considerate of her.

Howard broke the silence that had settled over them. He pulled a small black velvet box from his pants pocket and handed it to Ethel.

"Ethel, here is something I have been wanting to give you for a long time, ever since we met. Can you guess what it is?"

Ethel took the box as she looked into Howard's shining, adoring blue eyes. Opening it, she found a sparkling amethyst engagement ring, her birth stone, set on a slender gold band. Howard took the ring and tenderly placed it on her finger. "Ethel, will you marry me?" He leaned down and kissed her.

Ethel blushed, her head down, and looked at the ring on her finger for a long moment. Then Ethel looked up at him, and said with a twinkle in her eye, "I thought you'd never ask. Of course I will." He kissed her again and drew his sweetheart into his arms.

Remembering they had brought food, Ethel spread the red checkered cloth on the rocks and brought out the chicken sandwiches and potato salad as Howard poured tea from the thermos. They discussed a possible wedding date. Ethel said she'd like it to be in October, and that she wanted to be married in her home in Bucksport. Although that was only two months away, Ethel was sure she could be ready, and knew Mother would help.

Ethel was still in the clouds when she awakened early the next morning. She looked at the ring on her finger. So beautiful, exquisitely beautiful. She must tell Sara the news. Sara was stirring in her room, so Ethel slipped on her robe and knocked at her door. Sara, sleepy-eyed, opened the door to find the radiant Ethel, eyes beaming, hair streaming.

"Look, Sara, look." She held out her left hand. "Isn't it beautiful?"

Sara looked at the ring and then at Ethel. "Oh, Ethel, that's wonderful, simply wonderful. Now you'll be my sister as well as my friend. I am so happy for you, and for Howard too." She gave Ethel a big hug. "Tell me all about it when we get off work tonight." Ethel agreed and they both hurried to get ready for another busy day.

It dawned on Ethel later that morning that only single women were hired as teachers by the AMA, which meant she could not return

to Chandler. She must let Mr. Werking know immediately of her engagement so that he could get a replacement. She was sure both Mr.
and Mrs. Werking would be shocked, but also very happy for her. As
soon as her work was finished that evening she dashed off a note.

Dear Mr.and Mrs. Werking.

*You will be surprised to learn that I have become en-
gaged to Sara's brother Howard, and that I will not be returning to Chandler this fall. We plan to be married October
20. I thank you both for all your many kindnesses during the
year I was at Chandler. It was a great year for me, one that I
will never forget. Please give my special love to the other
teachers and to the children of Chandler.*

Kindest regards,

Ethel

While Ethel had no misgivings about marrying Howard, she
couldn't help but feel a twinge of regret that she would not be teaching at Chandler this year. She loved teaching. She'd loved the Werkings, the other teachers, and of course her students. She would surely
miss them all. She wondered if she were giving up teaching forever.
Would there be other opportunities in Maine for her to teach? She
was aware that in Maine single teachers were much preferred over
married ones.

Back at the farm the morning following their engagement, Howard was up early as usual to milk the cows before breakfast. The task
seemed to be lighter this morning, for his heart was thrilled at the

happenings of the day before. Ethel had said "Yes!" He could hardly believe his good fortune after suffering so many recent personal tragedies. As he milked old Betsy he tried to think of the words he would use to tell his Mother the news. She was in the kitchen now, preparing breakfast, making biscuits, scrambled eggs and oatmeal, and as usual, singing her hymns. As he came in the back door he could hear the words, "O Happy Day, Happy Day…" Oh yes, thought Howard, it is a happy day!

Howard washed his hands at the sink and slipped into his seat at the large wooden kitchen table. Mother placed the hot biscuits and eggs in front of him, and a steaming bowl of oatmeal with cream next to his glass of milk. The glow on his face told her he had something on his mind. He could not fool this discerning mother. "You look mighty happy this morning, son. You must have had a good time with Ethel yesterday." She carried her plate to the table and sat across from him, bowing her head to say her silent grace as she always did.

"Yes, Mother, I did. Ethel and I plan to be married in October. The twentieth." Like his father, Howard was a man of few words.

"I am very happy for you, Howard. Is there anything I can do for you or Ethel? The twentieth of October is not far away."

"There is just one thing I would like very much. I would love to have one of your patchwork quilts. You know Ethel has admired several that you've made. One of them would sure look nice in our new home."

"Of course, son. I can finish the one I am making now. That will be my wedding gift to you and Ethel. Or you might like to choose

157

one of the other ones I've made. Just select the one you and Ethel would like."

Nina Leighton was a little surprised when she learned that Howard would not be bringing his bride to live at the Leighton homestead, but she said nothing, knowing that Howard always thought things through and made wise decisions. She did hope that he and Ethel would live nearby. She wondered if he planned to continue working the farm, but of course she could not demand that of him. Did he have Maryland in mind for their future? She knew how much he had loved his job there. She would pray and wait and see.

Nina continued. "Ethel is a lovely girl, Howard. I am glad you have found each other. When are you bringing her back from Princess Point?"

"The hotel closes for the summer in a couple of weeks and I'll go up and get the girls, then drive Ethel up to Bucksport." He grinned. "Guess there is a lot for a girl to do to get ready to be married. And I'll have to pass the inspection of her Mother."

Howard was aware that in Maine a young man planning to be married only takes a bride when he has a house ready. And so the Sunday following their engagement Ethel and Howard drove around Cumberland Center and Portland looking at several houses for rent, hoping to find one they could afford. They came upon one in Cumberland Center, not far from the Leighton home, that they both liked. It was a two bedroom, two-story house with a cellar.

A neighbor across the street had the key and let them in. After looking around Howard and Ethel agreed that it suited them and they would rent it, although it had been empty for a while and needed repairs and painting. On returning the key to the neighbor Howard learned that the owner was Mr. Hamlen. The following week he gave Mr. Hamlen a month's rent.

Sara was happy about the wedding but disappointed that she would not be able to attend. She would be leaving by train for Lexington soon, as she had to be at Chandler in early September. Thrilled that Ethel had fallen in love with her brother, she took personal pleasure in the part she had played in bringing them together. Ethel's happiness was dampened somewhat at the thought that she must soon say goodbye to Sara; there was no telling when they would see each other again.

On the ride from Princess Point to the Leighton home, Ethel remembered the things she had left in her room at Chandler. Turning to Sara in the back seat she said, "Sara, you remember I left some of my clothes in my room at Chandler. And several books in my bookcase? Do you think you could mail them back to me? Send them to your home here C.O.D. and we can pick them up. On second thought, why don't you just send the books, and give the clothes to Mrs. Werking to sell in her store. I don't think I'll be needing any of them."

Alice Applebee Leighton (Schmidt) visits her birthplace, Cumberland Center, Maine in September, 1998. Author's collection

Chapter Fifteen - Mrs. Leighton and Mrs. Applebee

Ethel and Howard were thinking of the many things to be done before the wedding as they drove the miles from Princess Point to the Leighton homestead that afternoon. For Howard, there was painting, cleaning, varnishing the house, and buying of furniture and house-wares. Ethel had sewing to do, the wedding to plan, invitations to write, the house in Bucksport to be made ready for the ceremony. Ethel hoped she would be able to handle it all after the busy summer, but she was happy to be headed home. She had saved most of her earnings from the hotel job. How much did a wedding dress cost? Shoes to match, gloves, a hat, and the rest of her trousseau would probably take all the money she had. And then there were household items, dishes, curtains, linens, utensils they would need. Oh dear, perhaps they had miscalculated the time it would take to get ready for a wedding!

They arrived at the Leighton homestead about three o'clock. Howard unloaded their suitcases, and then went off to do farm chores. Mother Leighton greeted them with a warm smile.

"Your sisters are in the kitchen and very anxious to see you, Sara. Come in, Ethel. I can see you are both very tired." She urged Ethel to come into the homey, simply furnished living room. Taking both of Ethel's hands affectionately in hers, she said, "Ethel, Howard told me the good news. I am so glad you are to be married. You will be good for Howard. I've never seen him so happy. And it will be wonderful to have another daughter. Two daughters named Ethel."

Ethel sank down on the couch, heart warmed by Nina Leighton's loving welcome. Nina Leighton went into the kitchen and returned with a cup of tea and slices of homemade bread. Some of Ethel's anxiety lifted. When Ethel had emptied her cup, Nina suggested she go upstairs and take a nap before supper. She gladly obeyed, and sank gratefully into the featherbed. This feels like home. I love Howard's mother. I feel so at home with this family. How could I be so lucky?

Ethel admired this gentle farm woman, Howard's mother, with the kind smiling blue eyes, sensitive mouth, and soft fine brown hair. She liked her neat cotton house dress and white starched bibbed apron.

Howard had told Ethel how his mother ran the seventy-five acre farm as well as the house. The boys, Howard, Edward, Philip and Nathaniel, each had their assigned chores to do, cutting wood, caring for the cows, chickens, and pigs, planting the potatoes and corn. The three sisters, Mabel, Ethel, and Sara, helped the boys tend the garden, gathered the eggs, apples, strawberries, blueberries and raspberries, and worked in the kitchen with their mother when canning time came. Hundreds of glass jars lined the downstairs shelves, all filled with produce from their farm, insurance against the coming winter.

Ethel had learned from Howard about his mother, born Penina Ringer Wagner, one of fourteen children born to Thomas Henry and Hannah Catherine Wagner. When just a young woman she had left her home in Nova Scotia to find a job in Maine. She had been hired as housekeeper on the seventy-five acre Leighton homestead, "Wood-land" built by Howard's grandfather, Amos Leighton. There she had met and married one of the Leighton sons, Edgar Barton Leighton, a twin, in 1893.[54] Soon Ethel drifted off to sleep, dreaming of their eldest son, her fiance.

The 120 mile drive to Bucksport was beautiful. They drove up the coast, catching glimpses of the awesome ocean pounding the rugged rock shore. They crossed the river at Bath and saw the Bath Iron Works below them, one of the country's largest ship builders. They enjoyed the charming small fishing villages, Rockland, Rockport, and Camden. At Rockland the highway turned northward. They followed the road that paralleled the familiar Penobscot Bay, and then the narrower Penobscot River, and stopped at a lunchroom in Belfast. Finally they arrived at the dock where they boarded the small ferry that took them across to Bucksport. Enjoying every minute of the trip, they were exhilarated with the anticipation of the upcoming event. But for each, there was some apprehension as to how Mother Applebee would take the news of their engagement when they told her their plans. Would she approve?

Mabel Applebee had always been somewhat "straightlaced" in what she thought best for Ethel, and had kept a watchful eye on her daughter even into Ethel's adult years. Ethel sometimes resented this over-protectiveness but dared not make her feelings known to her mother. She wondered how her mother would react when told Ethel would not be returning to Chandler this fall, where she had been so happy. Yet at the same time Mabel Applebee would no doubt be glad to have her daughter back in Maine, even if it was in Portland instead of Bucksport, Ethel was sure of that. It was important to Ethel that her mother approve of Howard and concur with their plans to be married in October.

Charles D. Applebee, 80, father of Ethel V. Applebee, at Ethel's home in Rockville, Maryland, 1938.
Author's Collection

Soon they arrived at Ethel's home, a large three story white house on Broadway, with a bay window and a large lawn. Parking the car in the driveway near the barn, they ran up the front steps. Howard noticed similar houses exactly like Ethel's home on each side of hers. "Yoo hoo," called Ethel. "Is anybody home?"

They opened the door and walked down the hall to find Mabel Applebee sitting in the kitchen by the window, reading her Bible. When she saw them she closed her Bible and laid it on the table.

"Oh, Ethel, I didn't hear you drive in." She smiled at the two of them and seeing their radiant faces had the feeling she was about to hear some news.

"Look Mama, look what Howard gave me," Ethel blurted out, beaming. "What do you think of that?"

Mabel stood up to admire the ring and grasped its meaning. She kissed Ethel on the cheek, tears filling her eyes. "Wonderful, wonderful. I am so glad for both of you." She paused, looking as though she hoped it would not be too soon.

"Have you set the date?"

"We have been talking about October 20th. You'll help me get ready, won't you Mama?" replied Ethel excitedly. She searched her mother's face to detect any sign of disapproval.

"So soon?" Mabel was a little taken aback. "Of course, Ethel, I'll help all I can, and you have my blessing."

Looking at Howard, who had been standing behind Ethel and listening to the conversation, she said to him, "You'll take good care of my daughter, won't you Howard? She is the only one I have, you know." Her voice broke a little.

"Of course I will, Mrs. Applebee. You need have no fears about that."

Mabel was inwardly very pleased at this turn of events. Ethel was now 28 years old; suitors had not come beating on her door, even though she was both attractive and intelligent. To have Ethel marry as nice a young man as Howard seemed to be was a dream she had cherished for her daughter. Now it was about to happen!

"Come into the parlor, and I'll get supper on. It is so good to have you home. Howard, you must spend the night, and don't hurry home in the morning. We must get better acquainted."

As Howard and Ethel were sitting on the front steps that evening after the sun went down, Mabel called out the front door, "Don't forget what time it is, children," an obvious hint that they must not stay up too long. Howard pulled his gold watch from his watch pocket and handed it to Ethel. It had been his father's, and he prized it highly. Ethel noticed it said 9:30, slipped it into her apron pocket, and forgot to return it the next day.

Howard was up early the next morning and went into the kitchen. Mabel was getting breakfast. As Ethel had not yet appeared, Mabel took the opportunity to inquire of Howard about his family. She also wanted to know where he and Ethel planned to make their home.

"We've found a little house in Cumberland Center, not far from the farm. I'll still be helping my mother run the farm, I suppose, or perhaps I'll get a landscaping job in Portland. We have already rented the house. It needs fixing up, but I can do that in the next few weeks while Ethel is here."

Another matter weighed on Mabel's mind. "What church do you attend?"

"Our family attends the Congregational Church in Cumberland Center."

So this young man was a churchgoer. Obviously he was a man of character; any misgivings Mabel Applebee might have had were laid to rest.

Ethel lingered beside the Ford as Howard prepared to leave that morning. Howard promised Ethel he would write as often as he could, but insisted he would be quite busy getting their new home ready. She teasingly replied that she may not have time to write at all, with all the sewing she would have to do. Of course they did find time to write. Sometimes their letters crossed in the mail. It was just 6:00 a.m. when Howard headed his Model T toward home.

Chapter Sixteen - Love Letters

One of Howard's interests other than running the farm was the local Grange.[55] Meeting monthly in the Grange Hall, men discussed everything from education in the schools to the local fire department. Wives were allowed membership only with the approval of the committee. The evening after leaving Ethel, Howard attended a Grange meeting. On September 26, he wrote Ethel his first letter:

Dear Ethel,

As it is after eleven o'clock I will only write a short letter. Have just reached home from Grange. I turned in your application this evening. I am enclosing the money which I forgot to give you when I had the chance. I made very good time coming down from Bucksport, and reached here at one o'clock. I would have liked to have been there this evening. By the way, what became of my watch? If you still have it, and it is not too much trouble, please send it to me. Perhaps it would be best to have a new crystal put on first, so it is less likely to be broken. You can send it by mail.

It seems kind of lonesome here tonight without you but probably it will seem worse in a few days. I hope that you will have a good time while you are home. I have just had Mabel put a poultice on my neck. The boil doesn't seem to be so sore today. Mabel has finished her job at Williams, so is home now. I am going to get her to help me with the cleaning of the house. As it is late, I will close and write more next time.

Love, Howard

Ethel's brother Vinal was to marry Bernice Snowman in early October, and that wedding was also to be held at the Applebee home. That somewhat delayed Ethel's preparations for her own wedding. Her mother had a shower in their home for Bernice and Vinal on September 26, the day after Ethel arrived, which she described in her letter to Howard on September 27:

Dear Howard,

Expect you have been roaring around, asking "Is there any mail for me?" So there is, such as it is. We dolled up the house with flowers and autumn leaves yesterday and had the shower for the kids last night. We got quite excited when both the boat and the train came and nobody appeared. But finally Mrs. Buck telephoned and we found Clarence was bringing them. They got here about 7:30. The neighbors came in and a few from Orland, so we had quite a pleasant evening and they got some good presents. I made two kinds of little cakes and cocoa, then we had apples, fudge, and peanuts. The house looked sort of decent. We had the banister all banked in with red leaves and the table and curtains too trimmed up. Emma didn't come with Clarence, so he tried to make up with a pretty little Orland girl, then Sylvan thought he would cut him out and he asked to go home with her. She told him she had promised his brother, but Sylvan just grinned and told her not to pay any attention to that "fat fellow." When they left Sylvan and the girl were on the back seat and Clarence was alone in the front, driving Lizzie. All in the family! Suppose you reached home O.K. Hope Tarbox was on the job, otherwise you probably had a few things to say as well as to do. I went back to bed and slept till 8:30 after you left so with a cat nap in the afternoon I felt good as ever.

Must tell you a joke. Had to put Mrs. Snowman (Bernice's mother) in that room you had last night, so when Clarence came in late looking for a vacant bed he opened the door and looked in there. Mrs. Snowman thought Mama wanted her, so she sits up and says, "Yes, did you want me?" Clarence left immediately for the next floor, looking for sleeping quarters.

Oh, Howard, before I forget to tell you and you may be wondering about it, I am holding one bottle of iodine and one tin watch as security for that $4.70. Is that all you could think of to leave? What time did you get back? If you get any good pictures of our house don't forget to send me one.

Am going to get busy sewing right off. If you get those announcements done it will be all right for you to bring them, won't it? We can mail them any time after the rush is over and we'll have time to do it when you get me marooned on that little island. Won't we even keep a sea gull?

Am I now ready to become a member of the West Falmouth Grange or are there still sleuths on my trail? (Hit me)

Expect you had a pleasant trip for once on the way home as there was nobody to bother you. It is getting sort of lonesome around here now that the excitement is a bit over. Clarence went back to Dover this afternoon and Mrs. Snowman leaves tonight so it is going to be real quiet, I think.

Got to speed a bit as Mr. and Mrs. Vinal Applebee are downtown and I guess I had better help with supper.

Don't forget my name and address and hope you have written, but don't believe you had any time to do that Sunday evening. If you haven't time to read this right now save it till Sunday afternoon, but please don't say I didn't write as per order. Will write again when I get your letter. Remember me to your mother and everyone.

Goodbye till next time. Oh, the football boys are out in front of the house for practice! Seminary opened today. What became of all those kisses you gave me? Can't find any now. Be good and don't forget all my good advice and words of wisdom. With love,

Ethel

P.S. I mean Ethel Applebee. How's the boil?

The day after writing to Howard, Ethel opened up the Singer treadle sewing machine by the window in the dining room. It stayed open several days, as Ethel and her mother measured and cut and sewed her wardrobe and linens. She bought bolts of muslin to make sheets and pillow slips, and yards of broadcloth, percale and cotton to make several shirtwaists and long skirts. The customary ankle-length dresses were being replaced by the more fashionable shorter ones, that reached just below the calf. Since Ethel liked these much better than the longer dresses, her new wardrobe would go with the new fashion. In her next letter to Howard, she mentioned her sewing:

September 29, 1921

Dear U,

Your letter came today. I didn't expect you to write Monday night so it's all right if it wasn't very long. You must have my magazine by now. Have written to Sara and Jean tonight. Took the tin watch to the garage for the new windshield today. Will send it should I ever see it again. Have done a little sewing today. If it doesn't kill me shall probably do some more tomorrow. You better believe I love you when I tell you that sewing is not my strong point, and still I spend hours at it! Have to, you see, for I am so slow!

Thank you for the money. I wasn't at all worried. You see, I still have the watch!

That was rather nice what you said about treating me as you did so please may I say that I am glad you said it? Also, that I believe you would rather I told you. I think you are sort of decent to take what I told you on the Bangor road. 'Nuff said.

Wonder if you will go up "home" Sunday. Hope you will get some pictures if you do. Wrote so much last time that you mustn't expect much this time.

Do you realize that Saturday is October 1? I am afraid I am going to be afraid. Aren't you? I must quit and go to bed. Lots of love,

Ethel

Chapter Seventeen - The Fire

In addition to losing his father and his brother within the year, another tragedy struck Howard just three weeks before the day of the wedding. This time it was a fire. Howard described it in his letter of Friday, September 30:

Dear Ethel:

I received your interesting letter yesterday and expect another one today.

I had some hard luck last night. We had a fire which burned the barn and shed and all the stock. About the only thing we were able to save was the Ford and the top cart and one sleigh. We had a hard fight to save the house where the end of the shed nearest the house was full of wood and so near.

Mother woke up first and called me and said the barn was on fire. I wasn't more than a minute getting out but the fire was the whole length of the barn then and it was impossible to get inside to save any of the cows.

I had just time to get the Ford out as in less than five minutes the shed was on fire the entire length. We weren't over four or five minutes getting out the Ford and cart and sleigh, then we, that is, Tarbox and I, wet three blankets and I climbed on the roof of the house and spread them over the gable end and one on the roof. It was scorching hot by the time I reached the roof but I managed to stay there long enough to place the two blankets over the end. By that time the neighbors began to come. I couldn't stay on the roof any longer as I had no hat on and my head was aching terribly so I came down and one of the men took my place, and I began to carry things out of the house. They used all the water in the well keeping the blankets wet and the lower part of the house which was not covered by blankets. The worst time was when the end of the shed fell over towards the house but after a few minutes it was not so bad and we knew we were safe. We had just two or three pails of water left then.

About half the furniture was taken out of the house. Mabel turned in the alarm over the telephone at once just as soon as we woke up and of course the neighbors came as quickly as possible. Central notified the fire warden at West Falmouth at once or so she claims, but it was an hour and a half before he arrived with the chemical engine. It is built on a Ford, so should not take over ten minutes to reach here. He arrived after we had given up fighting and knew we were safe and used up twenty-five gallons of chemical. Stayed about an hour then went back and spread the report that he had saved the house. We are fortunate to have the house left. All we have left are the two colts which were in the pasture. I don't hardly know what to do about building. I suppose I shall have to build a place for the colts anyway. Have about twenty-five hundred dollars insurance on what was burned, but of course that won't begin to cover the loss.

I went to Portland this afternoon and purchased and brought home practically all the cooking utensils we will need. I got more aluminum ones than you said as there wasn't such a great difference in price. I got two aluminum kettles, double boiler and fry pan. I also bought two beds, one brass and one oak, but did not take them home. I found where I can get silk floss mattresses for fourteen dollars. Don't you think that reasonable. In regard to that cot bed, I think I shall send to Sears and Roebuck Co. for the one we spoke of. I saw one something like it yesterday and liked it fine.

I haven't found a hat rack and mirror yet that suited me. The price of all that I have seen is over twenty dollars. I saw a hall rack which I liked very much yesterday. It was one of those that have a seat in the bottom with a place for umbrellas at the side and was seven feet high and at least three feet wide. The mirror was eighteen inches by three feet and one-half, and it was a pretty piece of furniture. The price was forty dollars. How do you think you would like that?

I ordered those announcements engraved today and they will be ready in about ten days.

It sure is lonesome here now that you are gone. I will see you in twenty days, Ethel, and I guess I can stand it that long. I am going to keep that picture I have of you at least until I have you to look at, then perhaps I shall return it to its owner.

Today I had Tarbox, the hired man, load the beans on the rack and tomorrow I intend to thrash them. I have the colts but no harness to use. It seems strange not to have any chores to do.

With love,

Howard

Before she received Howard's letter telling about the fire, Ethel had written the following letter to Howard dated Sunday, October 2, 1921:

Dear Howard,

Have had two letters from you and you must have the same from me, but guess it won't do any harm to write again tonight.

Went to church this morning and it was not nearly so sleepy a service as it was last week. The Seminary students always attend and this was their first Sunday here this year. Rev. Cass had a solo and he is really good. Voice is bigger than he is.

This afternoon I called on that woman whom I waved at last Sunday, if you remember, also on another woman who is sick. I used to work for her when they were able to run a summer hotel. She is almost helpless now. I took her down all my Chandler pictures, including yours, as I knew she would be interested, for she is always very pleasant to me. She wants to see us. I think it would be decent of us to run in and see her as we are leaving town for she wants to see YOU and my clothes, and she may not live to see me again, so we will go in won't we? She's nice, won't scare you at all and she would appreciate it so much. She said you were good looking, but of course she had only the picture to look at.

Well, I suppose you have had a busy week. Did you go to Portland and if so I am anxious to know if you bought any "stuff" and what.

Has Mr. Hamlen finished the kitchen? You mustn't expect too much of Mabel, at least, don't work her to death.

This week when I haven't been writing letters to Cumberland Center and helping with housework have made up 50 yards of sheeting and have made a house dress. This week coming I am going to mend up my old clothes and make a quilt.

Vinal and Bernice are going to take some men by truck to Patten. They will camp and hunt there while the men go further into the woods for a week's hunting. They talk of going into the woods cooking this winter. That is, Vinal will do the cooking! She doesn't know how.

S'pose you will do the cooking?

Think twenty-five announcements will be enough for me. Can't count any friends above that number. If I do, will you let me borrow yours?

178

Hope you have your sleep made up so that you won't have to take a nap in the middle of the next letter I write.

The neighbors don't try to plague me any more than I thought they would so am standing it the best I can.

Have you told Ethel, Mabel and your mother that I expect them down? What do you want me to give you for a wedding present? If you have no choice I had planned to give you a roll of bandage for future use on boils. That all right?

Glad you aren't near enough to hit me! Guess I will stop before you try to. Write some time. 'Night, U!

Love from Ethel

Chapter Eighteen - More Love Letters

Ethel wrote immediately on hearing Howard's vivid account of the fire.

October 4, 1921

Dear Howard,

Your letter about the fire received yesterday. The loss of your animals and the barns as well as the shed was a terrible thing. And think what a loss I would have suffered if you had been hurt in the fire. Dare say I could not have stood it, to lose you, my dear. So glad the house was saved, and you still have a place to call home. I am sure your family and the neighbors too, know now, if they did not know before, what a hero you are. Were you thinking of me and your trip to Bucksport when you rescued the Ford? So glad you did.

You did not mention any change in our plans, so suppose you want me to proceed. But I can change them if you think necessary. You will have to be thinking about rebuilding the barn and other things. Please don't think you have to spend all your money on our home when you have those other things to replace.

Let me say I'm very glad also that your mother and brothers and sisters were not hurt in the fire. They seem like family to me now. Please give them my love.

You are in my thoughts and prayers every day. Can't wait to see you.[56]

Love, Ethel

Howard's letter written October 4 crossed Ethel's of the same date in the mail. He wrote:

Dear Ethel:

It's only a week ago yesterday since I left you in Bucksport but it seems like nearer a month. I was up to the house Sunday and Mr. Hamlen has finished work on the kitchen or at least he has put on two coats of light paint. It doesn't look bad but I wish I could get him to put on another coat. He has promised to have that old piano removed this week. The man that owns it called me up yesterday and wanted to sell it to me but I told him nothing doing. Ethel and Mabel are both home, and are going up Friday to do the cleaning.

I bought two quarts of varnish today and shall go over the stairs and some of the woodwork that needs it most. I took four pictures of the house Sunday and have sent in the film today. Saturday I sent in an order to Sears and Roebuck for that couch and hall mirror, hall stand and two chairs. They should be here in plenty of time.

I shall get the mattresses where I got the beds. $16.00 each for silk floss isn't so bad. There aren't so many things more to pick out now. There are those portiers and the art square for the living room, a couple more chairs, a book case *and set of dishes, that is about all that I think of. I think perhaps I can get Eddie to put up the silverware, and I think I know where a good lamp is coming from.*

There won't be any more wood that I can haul up as it will take about all there is left to run this house. I guess we will have to buy coal. It is lucky anyway that we have some left and I did haul up one load last week.

I was lucky one day last week. As I was riding along I saw what looked like a dollar bill in the road, so you can just bet I stopped and went back, and folded up together were four greenbacks and a few feet farther along two more. I kept on looking but that is all I could find. I haven't found an owner to them yet and I couldn't very well advertise so will probably keep them.

Ethel, I hadn't planned to tell you what I was going to give you for a present, but as you told me, I may as well tell you. Have been thinking of giving you a nice pair of earrings to go with that Dutch haircut you are going to get. Will that be all right?

I haven't decided yet where we are going on our trip. Have been thinking it over and thought I would like to see part of the state if we can. If this good weather holds out it wouldn't be too late. How would you like that?

I have made up a list that I ought to send announcements to, and have twenty-eight names but can cut them down to twenty-five, I guess.

I feel pretty near lost with no chores to do and I hardly know which way to turn. I lost all our tools so haven't even a hammer to work with. I shall keep Tarbox for a couple of weeks longer. We thrashed out eight bushels of good beans and I ran them through the winnowing machine today and cleaned them fine.

Mother and Ethel and Mabel are planning to go up with me. Eddie isn't sure yet whether he can go or not. Look Ethel, if it is going to make too much work for your mother, or if you haven't room in the house, the folks can stay in a hotel. How about it?

If I wrote the way you do what I have written would cover fifteen or twenty pages.
Goodnight Sweetheart,
Howard

The "bobbed" hair style that was coming into fashion in the early twenties did not tempt Ethel; she was not about to get her tresses cut, for she knew how much Howard loved her beautiful long hair, so earrings were not a consideration for her. Howard wrote Ethel again on October 6:

Dear Ethel:

Have had a couple of letters from you since I have written. Went to Lodge last night, so as it was after twelve when I got home did not write. I am attending Lodge regularly now as I don't suppose I shall have much chance after this month, will I?

Am planning to write to Rev. Cass tonight and ask him for one of those little booklets and of course I shall ask him to be on deck the twentieth.

I received a card yesterday from Loring, Short and Harmon saying that our announcements were ready. I will send you yours just as soon as I get them. Don't you think it will be best to have them all ready beforehand so all we will have to do will be to drop them in a post office somewhere?

I dug the potatoes yesterday and shall take up five to ten bushels the next time I go up to our house.

Saturday night I am invited to some kind of a party up at Cousin Hollis Leighton's. I guess it is someone's birthday. I don't seem to care a hurrah about going anywhere alone.

There is a church supper at West Falmouth next Thursday evening. Also Pomoma Grange at Cumberland Center day after tomorrow.

Ethel, just think, there are only two weeks more left. I'll see you two weeks from today.

I guess it will keep me hustling to have things ready up at the house. Ethel and Mabel are going up tomorrow and start cleaning the house.

There is a lot of red tape to be gone through with before I get my insurance. I have a paper more than a yard long to fill out in detail. I don't expect to get my insurance money in less than a couple of months.

Don't suppose I shall make a very long stop at Bucksport when I do go up. We ought to get started by four o'clock hadn't we? Would like to know what time you think we will be able to start so I can make my plans accordingly.

I suppose you have been getting a lot of (good) advice since you have been in Bucksport. I hope that watch does reach me in time for me to carry it back to Bucksport. I should receive those pictures tomorrow and if I do I suppose I shall have to write another letter tomorrow night in order to send you some. That will be too bad, won't it?

Do you have a lot of time for yourself so you can get your work done, or do you help a lot with the housework? Don't work too hard anyway, Ethel. I suppose you are having the nearest to a vacation that you have had this summer. I am not around to keep you up late nights. I don't suppose you miss me at all. Perhaps you miss the Ford, but I reckon you don't miss me at all.

With love,

Howard

Chapter Nineteen - Wedding Plans

With the wedding less than two weeks away and with many things yet to do, Ethel was getting nervous about finding a wedding dress. There would also have to be new gloves, hat, and shoes. Fortunately she still had money left from her earnings that summer at Princess Point. She had heard that Bangor had some fine dress shops. Why not ask Mother to go with her to Bangor to pick out her wedding dress? They could get the morning train up, spend the day shopping and come back on the afternoon express.

With most of the potatoes dug on the farm at Enfield, Ethel's father, Charles, had come down to Bucksport to be on hand for the wedding. He was a slender, handsome man of medium build, with dark wavy hair, a ready sense of humor and a twinkle in his blue eyes. He often said his daughter got her good looks from him. He did not take life half as seriously as his wife Mabel.

He had agreed to take his daughter and wife to the train station that Saturday morning for their shopping trip. Charles pulled the horse drawn wagon up to the platform. Mabel and Ethel climbed out.

"Meet us at 3:30, Charles, and don't be late," reminded Mabel as the train approached. He tipped his old felt hat and drove off.

What color should her dress be? What kind of material? Of course, gloves and shoes must match. Could she find what she wanted at the price she could afford to pay? Ethel mused as the train sped along toward Bangor, a historic town north of Bucksport, also set on the Penobscot River.

Mabel and Ethel visited several dress shops, and noted that most of the styles that year were in black, or black and white, beige or brown. These were much too somber for this bride-to-be. Blue was the favorite color of both Ethel and Howard, and she wanted to find something in blue if possible. Mabel was interested in rayon, a new material that year; georgette or chiffon were the other popular materials.[57] They could not find anything that appealed to Ethel until, after lunch, they wandered into a small dress shop on a side street. There Ethel saw what she'd been looking for.

In the middle of the floor was a manikin dressed in a straight dark blue dress. She hurried over to look more closely. The dress was of heavy rayon, trimmed with a black braid around the bottom of the long waist. The skirt hung a couple of inches below the calf. Wide sleeves, below the elbow, were trimmed with several rows of matching one-half inch black rayon braid. The neckline was plain and boat shaped. From the back of the shoulders hung a beautiful blue chiffon train, or surplice, the length of the dress. The stylish gloves of black leather were elbow length with a row of tiny buttons to the wrist. Dark blue suede shoes with a strap and buckle across the instep matched the dress. The hat topped off the outfit perfectly. It was of Navy blue velvet, with an ostrich plume on the left side of the brim. Ethel had found her wedding dress. The clerk and Mabel helped her try it on. Yes, they all exclaimed, it was made just for her! The image in the floor length mirror caused her to catch her breath. She was as beautiful as…a bride! Mabel looked Ethel up and down. "Lovely, Ethel, just lovely," she said softly, smiling broadly.

Ethel hoped she had enough money to buy the outfit, and she did. She paid the $47.94, ecstatic with joy. She couldn't wait to see the look on Howard's face as she walked down the aisle to become his wife.

Sunday afternoon, October 10, 1921 Ethel wrote:

Dear Howard,

Your letter received yesterday. Hope you have my decently written letter by now.

I took your watch to the other man here in town and he fixed it in about five minutes while I waited. I might send it this week if I think of it.

We went to Bangor yesterday and I came home penniless but happy. As usual I bought everything in sight while my money lasted. Mama has given me a lot of little handy things that I hadn't thought of before. She gave me a cute little covered dish that matches our pitcher. I kept telling her how much I liked it till today she told me I had better put it away with my things. Got your roll of bandage. Hope I get some of those pictures by tomorrow. It's a good idea to send the announcements. Just like your big head to think of that.

Yes, I think we ought to be able to get started away by four o'clock. You will have to wait till all the ladies kiss you and seems to me an hour of that will be enough unless you find you want a little more time to go around the second time.

My three neighbors will be here, two girl friends and maybe Emma, if Clarence brings her. Maybe three little boys in Francis' class whom I used to have in Sunday School. Guess that is all unless I think of somebody else. I want Mabel to help Bernice serve the home brew, if they will, after the ceremony. I wrote to Mabel last week. Vinal and Bernice aren't going on the hunting trip after all.

Don't worry about me working for goodness sake. I thought you knew me better than that. I never let anything interfere with my "getting ready" business and Mama is worse than I. She is always asking me if I hadn't better begin to pack. Whenever I was going away to teach she always would try to get me to pack a week before time. A week from today probably I shall be all ready, except my gloves, and be watching down the pike. If it is as cold as this you will have to put the side curtains on the Ford all right. What time do you expect to get here? S'pose you all may want an hour at least to rest and get dressed. Of course you can come earlier if you wish, only that will mean an early start from home. I probably won't know as much as I do now, by then, so I am trying to get everything said and done before I lose my mind entirely.

Anyway, I expect to finish everything except packing this week, then shall have the first of the week to do that, so the last day there will be nothing to do but walk the floor. (You might grin here or in other grinable places.)

Miss you? Nothing like I shall miss this letter writing. Did you have a big time at Hollis Leighton's? Aren't the leaves behaving well? Will you please keep them on till November 1? Just one place I insist on going that is to see the sick woman I wrote about. Yes, honest Injun? 'Gainst my principals to begin a fourth sheet of paper, so 'bye.

Lovingly, ME

Chapter Twenty - Howard and the House

The repairing and painting of the home for the newlyweds was nearing completion. Howard told of progress in his next letter to Ethel.

Sunday evening, October 10, 1921

Hello Sweetheart,

How are you? I miss you more on Sundays than at any other time. Strange, isn't it? I received the pictures yesterday and I will send you the three best ones. One of them is fairly decent, don't you think? Anyway, they are some better than the last ones.

I was up to the house Friday afternoon and put on some varnish. I covered the stairs and also the front room except the baseboard. Hope to get another wack at it this week. Ethel and Mabel did about all the cleaning except the windows and Ethel will go up some day this week and clean them.

Had a letter from Sears and Roebuck saying they couldn't ship my order for two weeks as they were out of mattresses for the couch. Do you think I had better cancel my order and get the things in Portland? I am planning to go to Portland Tuesday and Wednesday and I shall bring out the beds and mattresses and a lot of little things and I plan to have the goods from Carletons sent out sometime this week. I would like to have everything in shape by the fifteenth if possible.

This afternoon I went down to Deering and called on a cousin's family and had a very good time. Ethel, will it be alright to paint the stove with enamel or is it best to use blacking all over? I shall have to pick out those portiers this week, also the rug.

It sure will be fine to see you again, Sweetheart. I am counting the days now. Do you feel much afraid now or have you got over your fears?

Yours truly X X

H.

Rev. Walter H. Cass, Ethel's minister in Bucksport, replied to Howard's letter requesting him to perform the wedding ceremony. The letter was dated October 11, 1921.

Dear Mr. Leighton:

Your letter to hand yesterday, and in reply I beg to say, I shall be very glad to be at your service on Thursday, October 20th at 3:00 P.M. I enclose the booklet certificate which I will fill in at the time.

Remaining Yours faithfully,

Walter H. Cass[58]

Howard wrote to Ethel again on October 12.

Dearest Ethel,

I had a very nice letter from you yesterday and another one today. I only wish that I could write as nice long interesting letters as you do.

I was in Portland and got a few things that we will need. Bought that art square for the living room and the portiers. It was a hard job picking out the portiers and I don't know if you will like them or not. I had an idea that I could get them for four or five dollars a pair. I had to pay over twice that to get anything that looked decent. Bought the art square {wall hanging} and portiers {drapery for the doorway} at Libbys. I went to an auction of household goods at South Portland this afternoon and bought one of those sectional bookcases in oak. It is in five sections and looks like new and I got it for just about half what a new one costs. There was a complete oak chamber or bedroom set in fine shape which sold for twenty-two dollars for the set. There was a bed and spring and a fine large bureau and commode and stand. If we hadn't bought those things at Carltons I sure would have bought it. There were several trades in odd pieces in black walnut furniture, but most of that was junk. I brought that bookcase home and took it right up to the house.

By the way, Ethel, you are now a member of the Falmouth Grange. Last night the investigating committee turned in their report and I was surprised and gratified that you got by. I did not go up to Hollis Leighton's the other evening. It rained early in the evening and I did not feel much like going up there alone.

Haven't so many things to get now, only a set of dishes, two mattresses and a few small things. I wonder if I have forgotten anything. If you think of anything we need, please tell me.

We shall plan to leave here fairly early Thursday, probably around six o'clock. That should get me to Bucksport about one o'clock, if I have good luck. I don't want to hurry too much and I had rather be too early than late. I just wonder what you would think if I did not show up about three o'clock.

Say Ethel, if you keep on inviting folks you will have the whole of Bucksport there. Guess I will begin and invite all the folks I know. You know I am awful timid. You don't want to scare me so terribly do you. It's too bad that Vinal and the Mrs. will be there to laugh at us.

Had a good letter from Sara yesterday. I suppose that you have heard from her. She didn't say whether they missed you at all or not. Probably not.

I am glad that you finally did get the crystal put on my watch, although it is too bad that I put you to so much bother to have it done.

I am glad that you are getting along so well and have four days to pack in. I expect I shall be very busy up to the last minute and probably won't get everything done. I hope to put in one full day varnishing and something ought to be done to the kitchen floor.

Lots of love,

Howard

Chapter Twenty-One - News from Lexington

Back at Chandler Normal School, Lena, and Sara were indeed thinking of Ethel and the approaching wedding. Sara wrote Ethel two long letters, telling of their trip back to Chandler and the opening of school:

Lexington, Kentucky, October 2, 1921

Dear Ethel,

We had a fine trip. Our first excitement was at Boston where we waited a couple of hours for our train, and sat right there while it went out. The schedule was confusing and we missed our train by four minutes. The porter was very nice and took us to an especially nice ticket agent and he got us on another Pullman, but we had to wait another hour and a half to get it...

We got here about 9 o'clock and found no one at the station because, as we found later, they had just met the music teacher and taken her home. They met us in about 10 min. and we went home. We were just starved and the steak and mashed potatoes did taste good, also the lemon pie. Mr. Werking cut that and brought it to us himself.

We talked until about twelve, then went quietly to bed. Mrs. Smith, the music teacher, had already done so when we arrived. She is about Mrs. Werking's age and has been a music teacher for several years. She teaches piano, violin, mandolin and guitar. Some teacher, what?

Mrs. Werking is to have the chorus. Mrs. Smith will play for her. Mrs. Smith can't do very much with her left hand for if she overdoes it, it affects the nerve controlling the valve of the heart and sets her heart beating wildly. She says it's a nuisance but is said to be something that keeps on but does not kill.

The girl who was to take your place did not show up Thursday morning, and come to find out she was ill and had to be sent back to Washington for an operation. Her name is Maime Griggs and she was born in Portland, Maine. It is possible that the Anna Marie of which we have heard so much will come. If so, Lena will have to move into Kathe-rine's old room. K. is just the same as ever and is occupying your room. It was Lena's own suggestion that she move be-cause she said that Anna would not come if she had to be in that small room.

Cody B. is back. She is the one that bought your little silk hat. Your other clothes are all sold that you left here. Didn't you tell Mrs. Werking to sell them?

I haven't seen Harry Lee. He wasn't at school but is coming. Virginia and Myrtle are at Wilberforce. Rozell to another college. Cecil is going to teach at Taylor, Seales was sent to a college in Atlanta, sponsored by a white church of the same denomination for two years. They are providing for four months and he the other four. He was in to see us the night before he left.

Over the summer my room was used by the man who took care of the place and was "inhabited" when the Werkings got here. They soaked things in gasoline but neglected the couch cover. Anyway I was quite bitten up the first night so moved to Katherine's old room.

This room was turned topsy turvy, thoroughly cleaned, cover boiled and left for a few days. Last night I slept in peace in my old room. Am I stingy not to stay in K's old room? I don't know Anna Marie from a hole in the ground. I don't see how I could possibly stay there; you know how I mind the gas stove.

The Manual Training teacher has not showed up yet. I have only two twelfth grade girls and one, Alma Rogers, in eleventh...

We thought of you people at 9 o'clock Sunday morning. Please tell Vinal and Bernice that I hope they'll be one of the happiest couples in the world. How does the sewing come?

Lena, the Werkings and I went to church this morning. Mrs. was in the choir, the rest sat seven seats from the front. I almost went to sleep. The rest of the crowd are out riding now. The Ford is pretty old and rickety and won't hold six or seven anymore for a trip like the one to the river. I pleaded I had to write a letter so they let me stay at home.

Well, dear, it seems like a month since I saw you last, and I shan't say how I miss you. You know we have been together almost continually since October 1st last year. We are hoping to surprise the Mrs. this year by having a breakfast instead of a supper for her birthday October 8.

I'll write more school news later, when I know some more. Ella S., Helen, Marie and that bunch, Susie and Bessie, all asked after you. Let me hear from you soon, you sweet old lemon.

Forever your sister,

Sara

* * ** * * * * * * * *

Webster Hall

October 11, 1921

Dear Ethel,

I 'spect you think it's about time that I answered your letter. You don't know how good I am tonight. I could have put it off until tomorrow, since we have a holiday. The holiday came about this way. A nice looking fellow from a bakery called to sell me little pies and doughnuts and asked if we would be open tomorrow. I looked at him in amazement and asked him why we shouldn't be open, never dreaming that tomorrow was the twelfth. Then he went on to say that Booker T. and Russell schools were to be closed.

I came home and asked Mr. Werking, and he telephoned around to see if it was surely true that the other schools were to be closed, and as a result, the good news.

Mr. and Mrs. Werking, Mrs. Smith, Katherine and I went to High Bridge Sunday. It was a beautiful day and the cliffs were wonderful. Katherine and I went down and up the 359 stairs to the river bank. She has been all in since. I seem to be still alive and kicking.

Well, the new teacher has arrived. Just guess who it is? It is someone whose virtues were stretched to the gates of heaven, Anna Marie Hansen. She is over forty but is very quick and active in brains and in her physical being. She is just as jolly and full of fun as she can be.

Lena is to keep the 8th grade room with the exception of the arithmetic and one class of English. She would much rather have her room straight. Mr. W. will teach the arithmetic and Anna Marie the English.

Oh, I saw Robert T. tonight. He was out watching the boys practice football. I hear that he once wrote to Mr. Werking to ask to come back but I don't know whether Mr. W. answered it. Robert T. looks just great. He is darker than he was but he does not look as tall and bent over, for he has filled out so much. He weighs almost 175 pounds. Just think he is not yet 17 years of age. He is a splendid looking fellow.

My girls are just as bad and dear as ever. I had that 8th grade this afternoon. That Bessie and Fannie certainly are the limit, but I like both of them.

Nearly all of your pupils have enquired after Miss Apple or Miss App'bee. The first time that I saw Harry Lee he asked "Where's my teacher?" but chewed his words so that I had to ask him to repeat what he said. Then he asked, "Why didn't you bring my teacher back?" Richard isn't in yet. Many of the country boys have had to help with the tobacco and are just getting back now.

The Manual Training teacher comes the twentieth. He is said to be a fine band leader so I hope that we can have an orchestra, band or something.

Mr. Werking sent down to Transylvania University for a Physical Training teacher. The president said he could get us one quite easily. The other morning he called up and said that for the same price they would send us an instructor for the boys and a girl to teach our girls. The president added, "They are two of the finest young people that we have on the campus." We are very anxious to see them.

How is the sewing coming? I haven't had much of a chance at mine yet. How did you make the little pink dress? I'd like to see you in it this minute, and I can, almost. Your hair is all fluffy around your face, and your cheeks are all pink and your eyes shining and sparkling. And I'd like to have one of those embraces which you used to give me at night. I used to just love them. I suppose you hear from that brother of mine occasionally. I wrote to him last week and I do hope that he will answer me soon. But you know what brothers are.

Wasn't it horrible to think of the fire? I just can't bear to think of all of those animals being burned. It was really wonderful that they were able to save the house, especially where the wood was in the shed.

Lena is coloriting {dying} her old black straw hat. She has got to wear it until her check comes in. She says she is going to write when she has plenty of time because you always say that she doesn't say anything. I'm glad that I haven't got to wait until then.

Well dear, I expect to write again before the twentieth, but I want to say now how terribly, horribly glad I am for you and for him, and for me. Tell me all the news.

Much love, Sara[59]

P.S. Will send your books soon.

Chapter Twenty-Two - Wedding Preparations

Without evening chores to do, Howard filled the time by writing long letters to Ethel. He wrote again on Thursday evening, October 14:

Dear Ethel:

I have received two letters since I have written you. I received the watch yesterday and after all your care in wrapping it the crystal was broken. I am enclosing money to pay for crystal and postage, and thank you very much for bothering with it. I have mailed you the twenty-five announcements and you should receive them by the time you receive this. It is too bad that I did not know your father's middle name as it should have been used on the announcements. At the time I ordered them it was too late to wait for information from you. You said the letter was D. I think but you never told me the name. I had a letter from Rev. Cass and also one of those books called "Our Wedding."

You were wrong when you said in your last letter that one week from the time I read it that there wouldn't be any Ethel Applebee as I was reading that letter at half past one. I don't suppose it will do any good for me to say that I am sorry there won't be any Ethel A. as probably you wouldn't believe it anyway.

I have put in another day up at the house varnishing, and have cleaned out the cellar. I expect now that I shall have to let that order to Sears and Roebuck stand as they have my money and money is pretty scarce with me since the fire. I have purchased a new spare tire for Lizzie so as to be prepared next week. I shall have the furniture from Carletons sent out Monday or Tuesday anyway. I received a package from the jewelers today. Can you guess what was in it? Topsham Fair has been on all week but I did not have a chance to go. I am busy now building a place to store the carriages and tools in.

Ethel, it sure will seem good to see you again. I almost wish that it was all over, don't you. I guess I can stand it if you don't invite the whole town of Bucksport. We'll sure have to face the music when we do get back here. Nobody here knows the date yet except the folks. Probably I shall not write any more than two or three more letters to you.

Lots of love,

Howard

P.S. Gee, I sure would like to be where I could kiss you, dear. H.

* * * * * * * * * * *

It was a Sunday evening, October 16, in the Leighton homestead. Howard had just come in from caring for his colts and storing a few more bushels of potatoes in the lean-to shed he had built. Not having cows to milk now, he was restless on a Sunday evening. After washing up, he went to the desk and took out a few sheets of paper and a bottle of ink and pen to write Ethel. His mother sat in the rocker by the window, enjoying the brilliant red and gold fall leaves in the fading sunset.

"Have you finished the quilt you were working on, Mother?" asked Howard, "The one you're giving us for a wedding present?" He had not yet told Ethel about the quilt.

"I have just a little more hand stitching to do on it, and it will be finished. I'll bring it along when we go up for the wedding," she replied.

They had not had much time to talk lately, with Howard making trips into Portland to buy things for the new home and tending to the building on the farm.

"Where are you going for your honeymoon, Howard? I suppose you have your plans all made."

"Well, I thought we might drive through the western part of the state, and then to see the White Mountains. I'd like to take Ethel to Crawford Notch. They say it is beautiful there. There's a nice hotel, on a lake. I've only hinted to Ethel that we might drive in that direction. Want it to be a surprise."

"She is a lovely girl, Howard. I'm sure you two will be happy. When you get back from your trip be sure to come over and we'll have a big dinner together. Perhaps we'll invite some of the neighbors over, and of course Hans and Christiana Peterson and their daughter, Ethel. I see your brother Eddie is sweet on her. I wouldn't be surprised if we didn't have another wedding in the family before too long."

"Could be, Mother, it very well could be. Then there would be three Ethel Leightons!" Howard settled himself down to write:

Dear Ethel,

I received a letter yesterday but haven't had time to answer it before. We are going by Standard Time here since the first of October, so there won't be any confusion along that line. I am just getting over a boil so perhaps your bandages will come in handy after all. I shall be terribly rushed all this week and possibly I may find time to get down to Bucksport Thursday. I think we had better plan to be gone a week on our trip. What do you think? If it was earlier in the season I would like to take a month's trip. It sure has been warm here all this week and I only hope it continues that way for the next week or two. The leaves are still on the trees here.

I was up to Standish last evening for a load of apples and saw Eddie. He says he is not sure if he can get off for the twentieth. I hope he does. He is going to give us a set of silver. Did not go to church today as Rev. Jordan is on his vacation. He has gone to Washington. Tarbox got through last night, so I won't have him to worry about.

Probably I won't write you more than one more letter as it isn't such an awful long time to Thursday.

I forgot to put in the pay for fixing my watch, so will enclose a check in this one if I don't forget it. You are missing a lot of fun in getting the house ready. You ought to see me on my prayer bones varnishing the baseboards. Love, H.

Time was getting short; the days slipped by. On Monday, October 17, Ethel addressed her twenty-five wedding announcements. Howard planned to ask Ethel to help him with his; the farm work along with the painting, varnishing, and buying things for their home was taking most of his time. He would slip the list for his announcements into his pocket, and somewhere on their honeymoon they could address them.

On Tuesday evening Howard sat on the veranda steps, thinking over wedding plans. He was low on cash; there had been no milk or butter sales since the fire. The purchases for their house had depleted his savings. He did not plan to get a new suit for the wedding. He had that blue serge suit he had bought two years ago, and he only wore it on Sundays. That would have to do. His Sunday shoes still looked pretty good; he would get his little brother Nathaniel to polish them for him real good before he left. Mother would press his suit. There wasn't much he needed to take. He supposed Ethel would have a couple of trunks! He would take only the straw suitcase that had been his father's. A few white shirts and collars, underwear, ties and socks; that would about do it for him. And his straight razor. He would get his hair cut a couple of days before going to Bucksport. He hoped they would have good weather. He didn't want to have to take his heavy winter coat, and there probably wouldn't be room.

He was awfully glad he had purchased the rings back in August. He mustn't forget to take the ring. He hoped Ethel would be pleasantly surprised that they would be going to the White Mountains, and see Crawford Notch. He had always wanted to get over that way.

He wondered what Ethel's mother had given her for the house. Probably fancy things like doilies and table runners, pillowcases, and the like. He hoped Ethel would like what he had bought for the house. It had been fun fixing things up for her...

In Bucksport that week before the wedding, Ethel was going over her to-do list. Her sewing was finished and the new clothes packed in a small trunk; clothes and personal items for their honeymoon were already in a small suitcase.

In a second trunk were items for their house: several sheets, doilies, towels and pillowcases that Mother had given her, along with a few small little dishes and knickknacks. Oh, yes, and the rolling pin Father had brought her. There were her sewing things too, and her treasured school books. She would have to wait until they moved into their home to make the curtains.

Now the big job was to help Mother clean the house and arrange things for the wedding. The ceremony was set for 3:00 p.m. The minister and his wife would arrive about 1:30 and review with Howard and Ethel exactly what was to take place. While Ethel had not exactly invited everyone in town, she had posted a copy of the announcement of their wedding in the local post office, and knew that many friends and neighbors would come. There was also the matter of refreshments. Mrs. Buck, next door neighbor, and Mrs. Mann, another neighbor on their street, had promised to make cookies, and her mother would make the wedding cake and lemonade.

Ethel was happy when her longtime friend next door, Susie Buck, had agreed to be her maid of honor. She would have asked Lena, but she was in Kentucky. She would have liked for Sara to be in her wedding as well, but she was also in Kentucky.

Vinal and Bernice from Enfield, bringing brother Sylvan, would arrive about 1:00 so that Vinal, who was to be Best Man, would be there to rehearse the ceremony. Ethel hoped the crowd would fit into their living room and parlor.

Ethel decided on modest decorations. Bright yellow and red chrysanthemums would decorate the window sills in the parlor where the vows would be exchanged, and fall leaves would be entwined about the front staircase. She would ask Francis, her artistically inclined youngest brother, to help. She planned to carry a simple bouquet of white and red carnations. Howard would have a white carnation in his buttonhole. Oh dear, she did hope she wouldn't be too nervous and shake so much that Howard couldn't put the ring on her finger! She wondered where they were going on their honeymoon. Howard hadn't told her exactly.

Ethel looked forward to seeing Sylvan, her quiet brother who had stayed on the farm, and her older brother, Clarence, recently married to Emma. They would be driving up from Ellsworth. Howard would be bringing his mother and two sisters, Mabel and Ethel, with him. Howard's younger brothers, Philip and Nathaniel, would not be coming, but staying with a neighbor. Francis had agreed to greet the guests, take charge of luggage and gifts, and be generally useful in any way his Mother would dictate. Ethel hoped Francis would not go into any of his lengthy tall tales with the guests and hold up the wedding! Howard's two sisters would help serve the lemonade, and her mother would cut the wedding cake. At Francis' insistence, Ethel agreed to his cranking the gramophone to play the "Wedding March" as she appeared at the top of the stairs at 3 p.m.

According to Howard's letter, he wanted to leave for their trip by 4 o'clock, which Ethel thought hardly possible, with all the ladies wanting to kiss him, and the well-wishing of their many friends.

That, and the cutting of the cake, the opening of gifts, and the refreshments, would probably not allow them to leave until at least 5 or 6 o'clock. And then, Ethel really wanted to stop in to see her invalid neighbor, Mrs. Rice, at least long enough to show off her wonderful new husband.

**Sylvan Applebee, brother of Ethel V.
Applebee,
on the farm in Enfield, Maine.
EVA Collection**

Chapter Twenty-Three - Tomorrow We Wed

On the evening of October 19, Howard went to the house in Cumberland Center to make sure all was in place for his bride. As he locked the door he thought, "The next time I step through this door I'll be a married man. I suppose I can carry Ethel across the threshold. That should surprise her! I doubt that she weighs more than one hundred and ten."

On the way home Howard stopped to fill the gas tank and check the tires. After supper and chores he went to his room to pack. His mother had pressed his suit and starched his shirts and collars. He wrapped the precious ring in a handkerchief and tucked it in his suit vest pocket. It crossed his mind that this was his last night in this room; Phil had already asked if he could have it and wanted to move in the next day. Howard went to bed but did not sleep until the wee hours of the morning.

He got up early as usual to get his chores done; the old cow Betsy, bought from a neighbor, was especially reluctant to yield her milk, or maybe Howard was just a bit impatient. The girls and his mother were up for an early breakfast, all dressed and ready to go. Howard grabbed a glass of milk and a couple of hot biscuits, unable to settle himself down to eat a full breakfast. He was anxious to be on his way, so eager to see Ethel, so eager to take her as his wife. And a little nervous too, he had to admit.

Stops were made along the way to fill the car with gas and water. The Model T was an open car, and Mabel and Ethel worried about their hair blowing out of shape. Howard, grinning, assured them that they could primp and fix their hair on the ferry near Bucksport . It was quite a surprise to the girls to discover that the open ferry only carried two cars, a fact of course known to Howard.[60]

On the morning of October 20, Ethel also awakened early. Through the white lace curtains of her second-story window she noticed a soft rain was falling, although the weather was warm. To her knowledge, all was in readiness. Every room in the house, from top to bottom, even to the attic, had been cleaned and polished. Francis was to sleep in the attic so that Sylvan could have his room. She could hear Mother in the kitchen already. What a dear she had been! Helping in every way, sewing, scrubbing, cleaning, cooking. Ethel, too, had pushed herself to the limit over the past two weeks. She felt weary, yet excited with anticipation this morning. She just wanted to be with Howard, forever and ever. She allowed herself the luxury of lying in bed for an hour before getting up, thinking about him, their new home, their plans, and listening to the steadily falling rain outside. She hoped Howard would remember to put the side curtains on the Ford. Of course he would. That would be like him. "I wish the time would go quickly," she thought. "I wish three o'clock were here, right now. I wish Sara and Lena could be here. Wonder what they are doing at Chandler this morning?"

Suddenly she remembered the letter on her desk from Sara received a few days ago. Sitting on the edge of her bed, she read it again. It was filled with love and best wishes.

Rev. Cass, the minister who was to perform the ceremony, had dropped by the house two days before to talk with Ethel and Mabel. He asked Ethel if she was planning to have any music at the wedding. He said at weddings he performed he sometimes loaned his gramophone cylinder that played "The Wedding March," and he would be happy to allow Ethel to use it. Mabel Applebee brightened up immediately; she had so hoped there could be some music for Ethel's procession. Rev. Cass gave Mabel the cylinder, and she played a little of it. Ethel could hear it in her head now…"Here comes the bride…" This is October 20! I'm going to be married! She bounded out of bed and prepared for her wedding day.

Chapter Twenty-Four - Wedding Day

Ethel stood in the center of her room, all dressed and ready. Mabel Applebee gave her daughter a final pat of approval and hurried downstairs. When the chimes of the grandfather clock at the bottom of the stairs struck three, maid of honor Suzie Buck was to bring Ethel from her room to the top of the stairs. When Ethel appeared at the top of the stairway, Francis, watching from below, was to start the "Wedding March" and she would descend slowly, Suzie behind her. As Ethel stood waiting, there flashed across her mind thoughts of what she was leaving behind her—Chandler, teaching, her home, her family. But thoughts, too, of the step she was taking—marriage to a man she adored, a new home, and perhaps children. That first small step down the stairs was really a frightening step into the unknown, and she fervently hoped she would not regret it.

Suzie had helped her place the blue plumed velvet hat at just the right angle. She had pulled her wavy thick hair to the back of her neck and fastened it in a bun with hairpins. It was the only way she could wear it and have the hat fit just right. The hat picked up the blue in her eyes.

Her new camisole fit comfortably under her wedding dress, but Mother at first laced her corset too tightly and Ethel asked her to loosen it a bit. She loved her dress, and hoped Howard would too. She would soon know! The shorter dress was not nearly as cumbersome as those long dresses she had worn in Lexington. She felt quite stylish, ladylike; the surplice that hung loosely from her shoulders in the back was the touch that made it a wedding dress. She hoped she did not appear pretentious.

Her new French style suede shoes felt a little tight, but after all, she had never worn them before.

Downstairs, the crowd was moving into the folding chairs borrowed from the local funeral parlor for the occasion. They had been set up facing the bay window in the parlor, and spilled over into the living room that adjoined the dining room. There the wedding cake, white and glistening, waited on the center of the round oak table, which was now covered with Mother's best linen cloth. Two silver candlesticks held white candles on each side of the cake. Mother's best silverware and glasses were placed neatly around it.

Handsome Howard, his light brown hair combed back, looked stiff and nervous in his white starched collar. Beside him was black-haired, good-looking Vinal, the Best Man. They waited at the door leading from the kitchen to the parlor. When the music began they joined Rev. Cass at the bay window in the parlor.

Ethel had not seen her Father since early morning. He had declined to be in the ceremony, as "he didn't have a decent suit to wear." But Ethel felt sure he would appear somewhere on the edge of the crowd before the ceremony began.

Mother Leighton sat with daughters Ethel and Mabel on the sofa near the hall door, where the two girls could quickly slip out after the wedding to help serve the refreshments. Mabel Applebee, in her best black dress with white lace collar and cuffs, sat in the large formal chair on the left. Sylvan, Clarence, and Emma were on the front row, where Francis would join them.

The clock chimed three. Suzie beckoned for Ethel to come to the head of the stairs. Francis immediately started the gramophone and the strains of the "Wedding March" quieted the crowd as they waited for the bride to appear.

Ethel slowly descended the stairs, turned to her left, walked down the short hall and stopped momentarily at the door to the parlor. There was Howard, his blue eyes smiling at her, looking proud and happy. He watched her intently as she came toward him, between rows of neighbors, friends and family. Some gasped as she appeared; someone whispered, "How pretty she is." Out of the corner of her eye she could see Mother Applebee wiping a tear. And there standing be-hind her mother against the wall, hoping to be inconspicuous, was Papa, transfixed at the sight of his daughter, as though he were seeing her for the first time. Ethel's day was complete.

The Leightons, seated across the aisle, wore big, welcoming smiles.

As soon as the music ended, Rev. Cass, a small serious man with a high clerical collar, began to speak. When Howard stepped to her side and she took his arm, Ethel's nervousness left her. She felt his strength as he stood calmly there. He placed the gold band on her finger, smiling down at her. She wasn't trembling at all! Before ei-ther of them knew it they had said their "I do's," Howard kissed her lightly, and they turned to greet their guests as husband and wife.

Ethel remembered that day in a stanza of an original poem she wrote many years later:

> October twenty, twenty-one
>
> The friends have gathered in
>
> To see a neighbor girl in blue
>
> Become the bride of farmer lad
>
> Who from the fields of France
>
> Came back to make his family glad.
>
> Outside the sky is dull and gray
>
> The rain falls gently down
>
> Within is warmth and voices gay
>
> Gifts of linen, silver, glass
>
> Speak of wishes well
>
> Of those who in our memory last.[61]

As Ethel had expected, there were kisses for Howard from single guests which made him blush, kisses for her from friends and neighbors, hugs and well wishes. For the cutting of the cake the crowd dispersed to the dining room, some spilling over into the hall-way and kitchen. The bride and groom did not get away as soon as they had hoped, but finally pushed through the crowd and out the front door amidst showers of rice. Complying with Ethel's request to visit her invalid friend, before beginning their honeymoon, Howard stopped the Model T in front of the large old house with a wide ve-randa, grapevines climbing over the roof. Ethel, still in her wedding dress, knocked on the door, Howard standing shyly behind her. A voice called out, "Come in," and they stepped inside the parlor where a small, frail, gray-haired lady sat in a rocker with a colorful afghan around her knees.

"Oh Ethel, I'm so glad you've come. I have been expecting you." Mrs.Rice reached her arms up to Ethel for a hug. "And here is that young man you've been telling me about.

"So this is Howard. Handsome, like you said. You have found a gem in Ethel, young man. I'm sure you know that."

"Yes I do, Mrs. Rice. I feel very lucky that I found her."

Mrs. Rice motioned for them to be seated, but Ethel knew Howard wanted to be on their way.

"Thank you, but we must be going. We have a ways to travel, but I did want to keep my promise to you that we'd stop by." Howard was already moving toward the door. Ethel gave her friend another hug and a wave, and Mr. and Mrs. Leighton went hand in hand out the door and down the steps to their loaded, waiting car.

Howard headed westward, and on the way divulged his plan to Ethel. He had made reservations at a hotel in Augusta for the first night, as he knew Ethel would be tired from the long day. Then they would continue their honeymoon to the majestic White Mountains of New Hampshire, take in the Franconia Notch, see the Old Man of the Mountain, and then on to Crawford Notch where Howard had reserved a room for two nights. They would return the long way to view the Presidential Range, turn southward, then east to Maine and home. He showed her the route on his road map.

By the time they got to Augusta, the rain had stopped. The broken rain clouds were touched with rays of gold from the sun just setting over the distant blue mountains. It was a perfect ending to a perfect day.

Ethel the teacher becomes Ethel the housewife, 1923.
EVA Collection

Chapter Twenty-Five - Move to Maryland

Ethel and Howard settled into their little home in Cumberland Center. Howard divided his time between the farm and a part-time job with a landscape company in Portland. Ethel for the first time in her life was a housewife. She settled into her new role, but thought often of Chandler and the children there.

Howard was Master of the Grange, and Ethel occasionally went with him to the Grange meetings on Monday evenings.

The newlyweds soon discovered that honeymoons are not meant to last. One day Ethel, vexed with fixing Howard's clothes, got out her pen and ink and wrote a poem for him, which she entitled "Mend My Pants."

Now, Howard, dear, I must confess
Your clothes are always in a mess
Your buttons gone, your toes stick out,
And every day at me you shout,
"Oh, Ethel, can't you mend these pants?"
I patch and darn and sew and mend
Many a spare hour at this I spend,
I sew up rents, and darn your hose,
Sew on the buttons and press your clothes.
And then at night I hear

"Did you fix the pockets of those pants?"

And so I've searched and looked around

Until at last these pants I've found

They will not rip, nor run nor tear

Now trousers for me will be no care,

To me you need not say with anxious glance,

"Say, Ethel, when are you going to mend my pants?"

In February of 1922, Ethel was delighted to learn that she was pregnant and would give birth the following September. Blonde, blue-eyed Alice Applebee Leighton was born in Cumberland Center on September 10, and filled Ethel's days with many joyful hours.

**Howard M. and Ethel A. Leighton with daughter,
Alice, born Sept. 10, 1922.
EVA Collection**

Howard often recalled the short time he had worked for M. G. Coplen, owner of Rock Creek Nursery in Rockville, Maryland. (While there he had visited Washington, D. C. and had seen the exquisite cherry blossoms around the Tidal Basin, planted in 1912. Later, Howard was instrumental in Rock Creek Nursery planting blooming cherry trees at government buildings in Washington, D.C. and double blooming cherry trees in Somerset and Kenwood, Maryland.) Even though Howard had returned to Maine in February, 1920, when his father became ill, Mr. Coplen had assured Howard that the superintendent's job was his if he ever wanted to come to work for him again.

Having a family meant more financial responsibility. It was Howard's dream to go back to Maryland and take that job as superintendent of the nursery, and eventually to build a home. Ethel had known that this was a future possibility, but in the comfort of their little home and the joy of caring for little baby Alice, she never dreamed it was soon to become a reality.

In early 1923 Howard wrote to Mr. Coplen, accepting the job offer, and asking when he should come. Spring was the peak season for the nursery; Mr. Coplen wrote for him to come in April. The little family tearfully said goodbye to Maine, to relatives and friends, and headed the Model T Ford toward Maryland. They had to sell or leave behind much of their furniture and household goods, although Howard arranged before their departure to ship a large part of their belongings to the freight office in Rockville. Necessities like dishes, pots and pans, linens, and baby things were piled into the Model T back seat and loaded onto the running board.

Alice was almost eight months old but easy to manage on the three-day trip. At night they stopped in tourist homes along the way. Ethel tired easily on the trip, suffering morning sickness, for she was expecting again. Mr. Coplen had promised them a house on the edge of his property, located south of Rockville in the village of Montrose on Randolph Road.

The day they arrived in Maryland and saw the promised house was one of the saddest days of Ethel's life.

The house was a small, sparsely furnished, three-room house with a front porch and an outhouse. There were no close neighbors. Ethel felt like a foreigner in a strange land, a feeling that she never quite got over in the years to come. Her Maine accent, as in Kentucky, some-how set her apart; folks in Maryland knew right away she was not one of them.

A few yards up the cinder road that ran by their house was the B & O Railroad. The mournful whistle of the train that night as it passed the crossing took Ethel back to Enfield, the farm, her home, and Mother. Homesickness swept over her; she buried her face in her pillow and cried. When she arose the next morning she vowed they would go back to Maine as soon as they could.

A few months after their arrival Ethel had contacted a Dr. Linthi-cum in Rockville, three miles distant, and he told her she was to go to Montgomery General Hospital in Olney for her delivery. However, as her time for delivery became imminent, he wisely sent a midwife, an elderly Black woman, Aunt Laviney, who lived in Rockville, to stay with Ethel.

**Ethel Leighton Ricker, 21, sister of Howard M. Leighton.
EVA Collection**

On October 6, 1923, Howard went to work as usual. When he returned that evening Ethel, in bed, pulled back the blanket to show him his new offspring. What a surprise awaited him. There were two! Ethel named the twin girls Jean Francis and Eleanor Wagner. (Francis was her grandmother's maiden name, and Wagner was the maiden name of Howard's mother.)

Ethel was mighty glad to have Aunt Laviney around after the twins came. Then she had an idea. Why not send for Howard's sister, Ethel, just twenty-one, to come help her for a few weeks? She was not working at the time and agreed to come. She stayed through the winter. Pumping water by hand from the well, washing diapers by the dozen on the scrub board, fixing bottles and feeding three hungry little girls brought the two Ethels close together, and they became lifetime friends.

No doubt Howard sensed Ethel's disappointment and loneliness, for he made plans immediately to build their own home. Lots were being sold in a small subdivision in Montrose across the tracks. He picked out a quarter of an acre, and after putting a down payment on the property, placed his order for a $4,000 Sears Roebuck house, with basement. It was a "prefab" house; Howard erected it on the vacant lot. Ethel's brother, Sylvan, came for a few months to help.

The following year Howard contracted with a well-digger to drill a well next to the driveway, near the back door. The well supplied water not only to his growing family, but in days of drought it also supplied water to neighbors when their shallow, hand-dug wells ran dry.[62]

Ethel's homesickness and longing to return to Maine increased as the days passed, and since her sister-in-law was there to help her, she decided to go by train back to Bucksport for the summer while Howard finished building the house. They would take the train out of Union Station in Washington, D. C., change trains in Boston, and go on to Portland to visit for a few days with Howard's family, and then go on to Bucksport.

That plan was carried out, and both Ethels would often tell the tales of that trip, mother and aunt trying to manage three little girls in diapers on the train. Alice was not yet two; the twins were only nine months old and, as they were not yet walking, had to be carried. On August 24, Ethel wrote to Howard from Bucksport. He was on his way back to Maine to pick up his family. Addressing the letter to him at his Mother's home, she wrote on Sunday evening, August 24, 1924:

Dear Howard,

Your letter came last night. I wonder how far you are on the way and where you will sleep tonight. Probably you'll drive most all night through. Seems to me you must if you are to get here as soon as you plan. You will do pretty well to get here by Wednesday, seems to me.

You didn't say anything about the Bar Harbor trip nor what you intended to do with my trunk.

Hope the twins will be able to ride as you say, but they are awfully lively. Won't stay anywhere they are put, but roll over on their stomachs and squirm around. Won't stay on their backs as Alice did.

We had company today and one of them was sort of a fat man. Alice sat on his knee and persisted in calling him "Daddy." We had been telling her Daddy was coming to see her in an automobile so she thought you had arrived, I guess.

S'pose I'll have to get packed up this week. I have done quite a lot of sewing and colored Alice's white winter coat and fixed it up so it looks real well. Wonder if the babies will need winter coats to ride in?

You will stay here a night or two, won't you. You will need some sleep. Hope that you have had no trouble on the trip so far.

Well, let us know when to expect you and we will be here when you come.

Goodbye till I see you. Bet you won't know the twins. With love, Ethel

Howard M. Leighton with twins Eleanor and Jean, born October 6, 1923 in Rockville, Maryland.
EVA Collection

Epilogue

In their new Sears Roebuck home Ethel was happy. Over the years she found friends among the neighbors who moved in on Maple Avenue. Down the street were the Mansfields, and the Browns, and across the street the Rickettses, Broadhursts, Dombroskis, Crosses, Dupees, and later the Sawyers. Maywood Cross, who lived across the street, became a lifelong friend.

Howard continued to work as superintendent at Rock Creek Nursery. While living in the little house across the tracks, two ladies, Ellen Craigie and Mary Harmon, visited Ethel, inviting her to a little church that met at the Montrose School on Randolph Road. Lonely and wanting to make friends, Ethel and her family began to attend the services there. Ethel was pleased when they asked her to teach Sunday School. Over the years she taught several age levels—juniors, young people and senior adults—until she was past seventy-five. When the congregation decided to buy the lot next to their home and build a church, Howard volunteered, working many long evenings to help complete the small white frame building on the corner. When a parsonage was built later, pipes were run from Howard's well to supply it with water.

Later, Ethel substituted at Montrose School where their children attended, and she also served as P.T.A. president.

On August 1,1932, Howard and Ethel welcomed a son, Howard Noyes, into the world. His sister, Alice, almost ten, knew that he was the answer to her prayers, for she had often prayed for a little brother.

Over the years Howard and Ethel and their family made frequent trips to Maine, first in their Model T, then their Model A, and finally in their 1936 Ford, to visit family and to renew old friendships. Later Ethel returned to Maine to bury first her mother and then her father in the Applebee family cemetery in Enfield. Ethel's last trip to Maine was in 1970 when she was 77 years old, accompanied by her daughter Eleanor, son-in-law Floyd, and their three children, Floyd, Janice and Diane.

Sara Leighton taught at Chandler only one more year; in 1922 she moved back to Maine to teach in Yarmouth and then Freeport. Sara married Nelson Aikins in 1927, and their daughter, Sara Ellen, born December 22, 1940, also became a teacher. Lena remained at Chandler Normal School until it phased out the latter part of the twenties.[63] Professor and Mrs. Werking moved to Atlanta, Georgia. Lena stayed in the South, and in the 1940s, after the death of Mrs. Werking, she married "Fessor" in The Little Church off Times Square in New York City. Ethel once visited Lena in Atlanta, where Lena lived until past 80.

Ethel Applebee Leighton in Maine with her mother-in-law Nina W. Leighton, at Portland Head Light, Portland, Maine 1960. Author's Collection

When World War II came, Rock Creek Nursery, where Howard had worked so many years, was declared unessential to the war effort; gas for their trucks was unavailable. When the nursery closed Howard got a job with a roofing company, doing the heavy work of siding and roofing.

Howard died suddenly of a heart attack in Rockville, on January 20, 1950, at age 55. Because of his U.S. Army service in World War I, he was buried in Arlington National Cemetery.

The following lines, written by Ethel, are found in her book of poems, "Through the Years:"

'Tis winter and the night is dark;

The friends are staying late,

Our minds do not the hours mark

233

The husband, father, is no more.
Oh, Father, God, how can this be,
His hand no more shall open door
He'll speak no more, his voice is still
The silence deepens, clock ticks on
I cannot question the Father's will.

'Tis January twenty-four
The friends are standing by
To pay respects this one time more.
Last night alone we spoke goodbye
To him who once was part of us.
The organ peals, the song rings high,
That all the way my Savior leads me.
He through life has been my guide
He surely can my pathway see.

Now the soft breeze blows
The sun is bright,
The friends are standing 'round
The flag is held by comrades eight
And clear and sweet the buglar plays
The day is done and gone the sun
And there in peace our loved one lies.
A comfort in that folded flag
As close I hold it to my breast.

Yes, this my country while I live,

But there's a heav'nly rest,

And in that home beyond life's end

Will all our friends be gathered in

As sheaves to our great Savior, Friend

Who gave His life for you and me?

I thank Him for his love and care

Oh, let me true and faithful be

And to this home a few friends bear.

By Ethel Applebee Leighton (1950)

Ethel died peacefully in a nursing home in Olney, Maryland, on November 15, 1973, at age 80. Miss Apple was buried in Arlington National Cemetery beside her husband.

Ethel Applebee Leighton in her later years, ca. 1970, Rockville, Mary-land.
Author's Collection

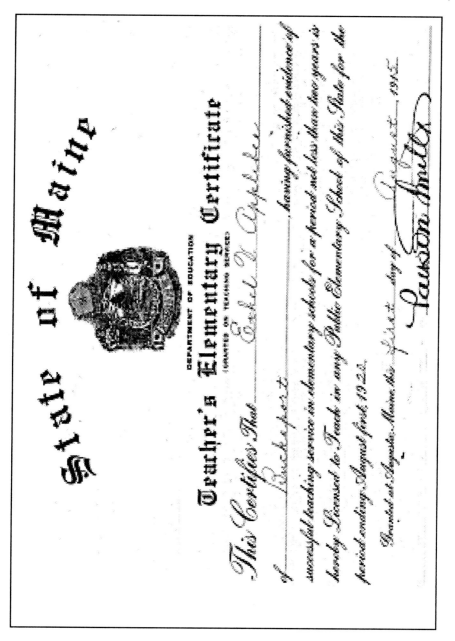

Teacher's Elementary Certificate, awarded Ethel V. Applebee of Bucksport, Maine, Augusta, August 1, 1915. EVA Collection

PRIMARY SOURCES

Letters from Ethel Valentine Applebee at Chandler Normal School, 548 Georgetown Street, Lexington, Kentucky, to Mabel Applebee, her mother, in Bucksport, Maine.

Letters dated: September 27, 1920, Undated, "Saturday," October 9, 1920, November 8, 1920, November 26, 1920, December 18, 1920, January 13, 1921, Undated, "Thursday Eve," January 23, 1921, February 13, 1921, March 5, 1921, April 1, 1921.

Letters from Howard M. Leighton of Cumberland Center, Maine, to Ethel V. Applebee, Bucksport, Maine. Letters dated: September 26, 1921, September 28, 1921, September 30, 1921, October 4, 1921, October 6, 1921, Sunday evening, undated, October 12, 1921, October 14, 1921.

Letters from Ethel V. Applebee of Bucksport, Maine, to Howard M. Leighton, Cumberland Center, Maine. Letters dated: September 27, 1921, September 27, 1921, September 29, 1921, October 10, 1921, Sunday P.M., undated.

Letter from Ethel A. Leighton in Bucksport, Maine, to Howard M. Leighton in Cumberland Center, Maine, dated August 24, 1924.

Two letters from Sara E. Leighton, Lexington, Kentucky, to Ethel V. Applebee in Bucksport, Maine, dated October 2, 1921 and October 11, 1921.

Letter of Rev. E. S. Burrill, Supt. of Schools, Sebec Village, Maine, to Ethel Applebee, Mt. Kineo House, Maine, dated August 7, 1911.

Story: "The Purchased Possession," by Ethel A. Leighton.

Letter of Rev. Walter H. Cass, Bucksport, Maine, to Howard M. Leighton of Cumberland Center, Maine, dated October 11, 1921.

Through the Years, by Ethel A.Leighton, book of poetry, self-published, 1965, Bernard Dorff, Publisher, Baltimore, MD.

"Mend My Pants," by Ethel A. Leighton, Cumberland Center, Maine, for Howard M. Leighton, 1923.

"Making Connections," unpublished article by Jean L. Testerman, daughter of Howard and Ethel Leighton, about Howard M. Leighton.

Letter from Ethel L. Ricker, September 19, 1989, sister of Howard M. Leighton, describing trip from Cumberland Center to Bucksport for the wedding, to Alice A. Schmidt, of Rockville, Maryland, daughter of Howard and Ethel Leighton.

Letter from Laura Carroll December 17, 1936, to Sara Leighton Aikins from Lexington, Kentucky.

Excerpts from photocopy of *Observer and Reporter*, Lexington, Kentucky, June 26, 1867: "Negro school in old city hall… and taught by 1 male and several females, sent here from the North and paid in large part by some Northern society."

Excerpts from photocopies of *Lexington Leader*, newspaper of Lexington, Kentucky, as follows:
    May 12, 1895, page 10, column 3, 4, Temperance taught at Chandler Normal School, located on Georgetown Pike.

    June 14, 1895, page 8, column 3, Chandler Normal School closes its year; creditable closing exercises of the various departments. "A colored institution that is doing a splendid educational work."

Excerpts from photocopies of newspaper *Lexington Leader* published in Lexington, Kentucky, as follows:
    May 16, 1886, page 4, column 3, House Legislature votes to establish a Normal School, allots $7,000 for building, $3,000 annually for expenses.

    October 17, 1886, page 2, column 1, Lexington County to vote on giving land for colored Normal School.

    October 25, 1888, page 4, column 4, American Missionary Association raising funds.

January 14, 1890, page 8, column 4, $15,000 donated by Mrs. Phoebe Chandler for building, cost $10,000; description of school and campus.

February 11, 1890, page 2, column 3, Dedication of Chandler Normal School and formally tendered to the colored people of Lexington by C. W. Hyatt, Secretary of the American Missionary Association, a gift of Mrs. Phoebe Chandler.

June 6, 1892, page 7, column 3, Colored teachers adopt Resolution of Appreciation to Mr. M. A. Cassidy, Superintendent of Lexington Schools, signed by 16 colored teachers.

June 8, 1892, page 3, column 3, Chandler Graduation Exercises.

June 13, 1894, page 4, column 4, The Colored Normal School closes successful year. "A splendid institution for higher education of the colored race," Mrs. Shaw, principal.

June 1, 1896, page 5, column 3, Anniversary Week of Chandler School, speeches, recitals, awards, graduation.

June 5, 1898, page 3, column 1, 2, Chandler Normal School Commencement; unveiling of the picture of the donor, Mrs. Phoebe A. Chandler.

May 28, 1900, page 7, column 4, Chandler Normal School Commencement, sermon and musical program, Miss Webster, principal.

June 3, 1900, page 3, column 1, 5, "In 1889 the school moved to its present excellent building, the gift of Mrs. Chandler, and took the name of its benefactor."

SECONDARY SOURCES

Beard, Augustus Field. *A Crusade of Brotherhood: A History of the American Missionary Association.* Boston: Pilgrim Press, 1909.

Brooks, Phillips. *The Beauty of a Life of Service.* Philadelphia: The Henry Altemus Company, 1896.

Clinton, Catherine. *The Other Civil War: American Women in the Nineteenth Century.* New York: Hill and Wang, 1986.

Fouse, William H. "Educational History of the Negroes of Lexington, Kentucky," M.Ed. thesis, Teachers College, University of Cincinnati, 1937.

Litwack, Leon F. *Been in the Storm So Long.* New York: Vantage Books, 1979.

Litwack. *North of Slavery, The Negro in the Free States, 1790-1860.* Chicago: University of Chicago Press, 1961.

Reilly, Wayne E., Editor. *Sarah Jane Foster, Teacher of the Freedmen, A Diary and Letters.* Charlottesville and London: University Press of Virginia, 1990.

Richardson, Joe M. *Christian Reconstruction: The American Missionary Association and Southern Blacks, 1861-1890.* Athens: University of Georgia Press, 1986.

Wright, George C. *A History of Blacks in Kentucky.* Vol. 2: *In Pursuit of Equality, 1890-1980.* Lexington, Kentucky: The Kentucky Historical Society, n.d.

Wright, John D., Jr. *Lexington, Heart of the Bluegrass.* Lexington, Kentucky: Lexington-Fayette County Historic Commission, 1982.

Report and Statement of School Committee for 1911-1912, Sebec Village, listing Ethel Applebee as teacher.

Plat of Town of Sebec, Maine, 1880, showing location of seven schools.

Map of town of Bucksport Village, Maine, showing four houses built by Joseph L. Buck on Broadway, 1881.

Letter from Elizabeth Ellis of the Sebec Village Historical Society, June 14, 1998, to author, describing school locations, and the Harriman School, now a museum, similar to school No.7 at which Ethel Applebee taught.

Directory of Teachers in Service, Aroostook County, Maine, March 1, 1918, and March 1, 1919, listing the name of Ethel Applebee as teacher at Fuller School at a salary of $14.00 per week.

Papers and photo from American Missionary Association archives, Amistad Research Center, Tulane University, New Orleans, Louisiana.

INTERVIEWS

Dwight Fuller (Eleanor Cunningham, January, 1998), student of Ethel V. Applebee when she taught at Fuller School in Easton, Maine in 1917-1920.

Philip Noyes Leighton (Eleanor Cunningham, 1998), brother of Howard Leighton, at Westbrook, Maine.

Max Place (Eleanor Cunningham, 1998), attended school in Sebec, Maine, about 1911-1915.

Elizabeth Ellis, (Eleanor Cunningham, 1998), member of the Sebec Historical Society, Sebec, Maine. (On occasion of visit to Harriman School Museum, Sebec Village, Maine).

End Notes

Historical Background

[1] Carson Clayborne, ed., *The Autobiography of Martin Luther King, Jr.* (New York: Warner Books, Time Warner Company, 1998), 105.

[2] Catherine Clinton, *The Other Civil War: American Women in the Nineteenth Century*, rev. ed. (New York: Hill and Wang, 1984), 123.

[3] John D. Wright, Jr., *Lexington: Heart of the Bluegrass* (Lexington and Fayette County Historical Commission, 1982), 119, and "Weldon Writes of the Chandler Normal Commencement," *Lexington Leader*, June 5, 1898.

[4] Joe M. Richardson, *Christian Reconstruction: The American Missionary Association and Southern Blacks, 1861-1890* (Athens, GA: University of Georgia Press, 1986), 135.

[5] August Meier and Elliott Rudwick, *From Plantation to Ghetto*, rev. ed. (New York: Hill and Wang 1970), 201.

6 Andrew Ward, *Dark Midnight When I Rise: The Story of the Jubilee Singers Who Introduced the World to the Music of Black America* (New York: Farrar, Straus and Giroux, 2000), 180-181.

[7] Leon F. Litwack, *Been in the Storm So Long: The Aftermath of Slavery* (New York: Vantage Books, 1979), 452.

[8] Litwack, *Been in the Storm*, 453.

[9] Meier and Rudwick, *From Plantation to Ghetto*, 207-208.

[10] Richardson, *Christian Reconstruction*, 135.

[11] Richardson, *Christian Reconstruction*, 163.

[12] Litwack, *Been in the Storm*, 453.

[13] Wright, *Lexington,* 119.

[14] F. J. Webster, *Chandler Normal School - An Interesting Institution* (New York: American Missionary Association, 1902), 2.

[15] George C. Wright, *A History of Blacks in Kentucky*, Volume 2, 119.

Chapters 1-25

[1] Phillips Brooks, *The Beauty of A Life of Service*, 26.

[2] Ethel Applebee, "Valedictory Address," June 14, 1911.

[3] Letter from Rev. E. S. Burrill to Ethel Applebee, August 7, 1911.

[4] 1880 Map, Town of Sebec, Maine.

[5] Max Place, "Max Place recalls Sebec Station School," Sebec Village, Maine, *Newsletter*, May 25, 1998, 7...

[6] Hazel Hall and Laura Hall Dunham, *No, We Weren't Poor, We Just Didn't Have Any Money* (Ann Arbor, MI: Braun-Brumfield, 1993), 2, 37.

[7] Interview with Dwight Fuller, February, 1998.

[8] Letter from Clarence Applebee to Francis Applebee, December 16, 1918.

[9] Richardson, *Christian Reconstruction,* p. 42. Subjects included reading, writing, arithmetic, spelling, grammar, geography, singing, history, Bible, and prayer.

[10] Interview with Dwight Fuller, February, 1998.

[11] Muriel deBonaventura. Genealogy Chart., n.d.

[12] Augustus F. Beard. *A Crusade of Brotherhood* (New York: Pilgrim Press, 1909), 317.

[13] That Chandler School was for prominent African American children is mentioned in Isabelle Mack-Overstreet, *Heritage: The Lexington African-American Discovery Guide* ([Lexington, KY]: n.p., 1996), no pagination.

[14] Ethel Applebee Leighton, "The Purchased Possession," article, 1941.

[15] Richardson, *Christian Reconstruction,* 166.

[16] Sara Leighton Aikins' resume, listing salary at Chandler, 1920-1922, as $1000 annually, including room and board.

[17] *Lexington Leader*, September 30, 1920.

[18] Peter Dow Bachelder, Mason Philip Smith, *Four Short Blasts* (Portland, Maine: Provincial Press, 1998) 10.

[19] Leon F. Litwack, *North of Slavery, the Negroes in the Free States 1790-1860* (Chicago: University of Chicago Press, 1970), 25.

[20] *Lexington Leader*, January 14, 1890.

[21] *Lexington Leader*, June 5, 1898, photo of Phoebe Chandler presented to school.

[22] Lexington Leader, January14, 1890.

[23] *Lexington Leader*, May 30, 1920.

[24] Ethel V. Applebee, Diploma awarded from East Maine Conference Seminary, normal school, June 14, 1911; Elementary Teaching

Certificate, State of Maine, August 1, 1915; Sara Leighton, Farmington State Normal School, Farmington, Maine, 1920.

[25] Sara Leighton's letter from Lexington, Kentucky to Ethel Applebee, Bucksport, Maine dated October 2, 1921, used by permission of daughter, Sally Dunham.

[26] *Lexington Leader*, October 25, 1888; February 11, 1890.

[27] Catherine Clinton, *The Other Civil War*, 88.

[28] Richardson, *Christian Reconstruction*, 43.

[29] Richardson, *Christian Reconstruction*, 46-47.

[30] Litwack, *Been in the Storm So Long*, 453.

[31] Richardson, *Christian Reconstruction*, 47.

[32] Laura Carroll letter of December 17, 1936 from Lexington, Kentucky, to Sara Leighton Aikins and newspaper clipping from Lexington, Kentucky, stating Laura Carroll taught at Chandler School from 1907-1929, and died in 1939, and that a public library was named for her.

[33] William H. Fouse, "Educational History of the Negroes of Lexington, Kentucky," dissertation, University of Cincinnati, 1937, 72-73.

[34] The name of Maggie Smith appears in early editions of the *Lexington Leader*. Two black teachers appear in photograph at Chandler, 1920-21.

[35] Loyal Temperance Legion and Woman's Christian Temperance Union.

[36] *Lexington Leader*, May 12, 1895.

[37] "Rules of Demorest Speech Contests," *Lexington Leader*, May 12, 1895.

[38] Ethel Valentine Applebee (my mother) lived in that historical era when the reciting of poetry was encouraged, and elocution a highly respected art. Later she would recite such poems to her four children.

[39] Ethel's brother, Clarence, had bad eyes from being gassed while in the Army, WWI.

[40] This is a reference to Fort Fairfield, a town in the far north of Maine where, because of location, no teacher ever wanted to go.

[41] Beard, *A Crusade of Brotherhood*, p. 222.

[42] Sara Leighton's resume giving salary while at Chandler. This was a higher wage than paid in public schools, which paid an average weekly salary of $12.83 in the South in 1928. See Irving Bernstein, *The Lean Years, A History of the American Worker 1920-1930* (Baltimore: Penguin, 1970), 10.

[43] Clinton, *The Other Civil* War, 122-125. Thousands of northern teachers went south after the Civil War. Many were rejected by both blacks and whites in the South.

[44] A true story told by Ethel Applebee Leighton to her daughter, Jean Leighton Testerman, in the later years of Ethel's life.

[45] John Thompson, "Mammoth Cave, Kentucky" booklet (1909), 3, 4.

[46] Fouse, "Educational History," p. 109. Chandler Normal School was closed in 1923 when Dunbar High School was nearing completion.

[47] The commencement exercises here described appeared in the *Lexington Leader* on June 8, 1892. Other reports of similar exercises

were reported in the June 13, 1894 and June1, 1896 issues of the *Lexington Leader*.

[48] *Lexington Leader* article of May 12, 1895, describes the Demorest Speech Contest which was part of the closing exercises for the year.

[49] There was some doubt as to whether Chandler would remain open the next year. See *Lexington Leader* September 13, 1920 and September 30, 1920. "Friends are gratified to learn that it will continue as it has for nearly half a century."

[50] Philip Leighton, brother of Howard, at age 88, told this story of the tragic death of their brother Wilfred, December 12, 1920 at Cumberland Center, Maine, in an interview with Eleanor Cunningham in September, 1998.

[51] Philip Leighton wrote this statement in a letter to Eleanor Cunningham, his niece, in February, 1998.

[52] Leighton genealogy, Leighton Descendants of Amos Leighton, Woodland Farm, Falmouth, Maine, by Philip Leighton, Westbrook, Maine, p 4.

[53] Philip Leighton, letter to Eleanor Cunningham, his niece, dated February 1998, "Howard had bought a Model T Ford and drove up to see Ethel quite often."

[54] Leighton genealogy, Leighton Descendants of Amos Leighton, Woodland Farm, Falmouth, Maine, p. 4. Penina Ringer Wagner, born at Port Mouton, Nova Scotia September 19, 1874, died at Portland, Maine April 6, 1970.

[55] The Grange was a farmers' organization, mostly in the northeastern and northwestern states which worked with the Department of Agriculture and with state departments to spread farm education and help the welfare of the farmer. Many local granges built their own halls for meetings and recreation.

[56] The letter that Ethel Applebee wrote to Howard Leighton in response to his letter about the fire could not be located, so the author took the liberty to imagine this letter as Ethel would have written it.

[57] Jane Mulvagh, *Vogue Fashion History of the Twentieth Century* (New York: Viking Press, 1988), 66.

[58] Letter from Rev. Walter H. Cass to Howard Leighton dated October 11, 1921.

[59] Two letters from Sara Leighton in Lexington, Kentucky to Ethel Applebee in Bucksport, Maine, dated October 2, 1921 and October 11, 1921. Used by permission of Sally Dunham, daughter of Sara Leighton.

[60] Ethel Leighton Ricker of Falmouth, Maine, describes this trip in a letter dated September 19, 1989, to Alice Applebee Schmidt, niece, of Rockville, Maryland. Used by permission of Alice Schmidt.

[61] From poem entitled "Friends," from *Through the Years*, a self-published book of poems by Ethel Applebee Leighton, 1965.

[62] Eleanor Cunningham, "Dad's Well," *Gaithersburg Gazette*, September 19, 1997.

[63] Wright, *Lexington*. "The new high school for Negroes was completed in 1923, named for Paul Lawrence Dunbar. It spelled the demise of Chandler Normal School, which gradually phased out its curriculum and by 1926 was used as a training school for men and boys who wished to learn a trade in furniture making and repair. It also maintained a kindergarten," 176.

Directory of Teachers in Service March 1, 1919

School	Teachers	Salaries	Grade or Subjects	Residence
High	Geo. H. Beard	$1,400.00 per year	Math and Science	Ackworth, N. H.
High	Inez Robinson	750.00 "	Latin, French, English	Island Falls, Me.
High	Donavilla Bishop	700.00 "	English and Home Economics	Auburn, Me.
High	David Hoyt	504.00 "	Commercial	Easton, Me.
Easton Gram.	Ellen Mahaney	16.00 per week	V, VI, VII, VIII	Easton, Me.
Easton Prin.	Lois Randall	15.00 "	I, II, III, IV	Easton, Me.
Center	Ula Bond	15.00 "	Rural	Monticello, Me.
Curtis	Grace McKinney	16.00 "	"	Fort Fairfield, Me.
Doling	Hope McKinney	14.00 "	"	Fort Fairfield, Me.
Fuller	Ethel Applebee	15.00 "	"	Bucksport, Me.
Getchell	Birdie Ireland	15.00 "	"	Presque Isle, Me.
Ladner	Florence Flewelling	11.00 "	"	Easton, Me.
Mahany	Marguerite Child	15.00 "	"	Easton, Me.
McManus	Freedom Hummel	14.00 "	"	Easton, Me.
Pine Tree	Doris Thompson	14.00 "	"	Easton, Me.

Directory of Teachers in Service March 1, 1919, Easton, Maine, lists Ethel Applebee as teacher at the Fuller School.
Courtesy Maine State Library, Augusta, Maine

About the Author

Eleanor Cunningham was born and reared in Rockville, Maryland. After high school she chose a business career, and graduated in 1941 with honors from Temple Secretarial School in Washington, D.C. While a school secretary, her collection of poems, *This Place: Love Letters to a School*, was published by the Montgomery County Public Schools.

Always a lover of history, Eleanor has published several historical pieces. Her essay, "Dad's Well" was runner up in the Maryland: You are Beautiful writing contest for senior citizens in 1990, and it was later published by the Montgomery County Historical Society. She wrote an article for the *Montgomery Journal* in 1997 on the occasion of the grand reopening of tiny Montrose School, "Montrose School: Back to Its Roots as Teachers and Students Return."

Miss Apple is Eleanor Cunningham's fourth book. Eleanor entered a Christian writer's contest at Warner Press, Anderson, Indiana. Her book, *He Touched Her*, won second prize and was published in 1973. Peerless Rockville, the preservation organization that saved and restored Montrose School, asked Eleanor to write a history of the school she attended in the 1920s and 30s. Her book, *Montrose School: The First Ninety Years*, was published by Peerless Rockville in December, 1999. In 2000, she published a *History of the*

Gaithersburg Church of the Nazarene on the occasion of its fortieth anniversary.

Over the years she has volunteered at Gaithersburg HELP, the Recovery Thrift Shop, and as a second grade tutor. As missions director at her church she led three work teams to Paraguay and the Philippines, and has enjoyed teaching both children and adults in Sunday school. She is a member of a weekly writer's group at the local senior center. She and her husband Floyd, now deceased, had three children, Floyd Timothy, Janice Ethel, and Diane Kathleen. She has one grandson, Ethan Wesley Leclerc.

Eleanor Cunningham is retired and lives in Gaithersburg, Maryland.

Printed in the United States
1322400005B/67-90